The Best of Brownie Stories

The Best of
BROWNIE
Stories

Purnell

SBN 361 04180 2

Published 1978 by Purnell Books, Berkshire House, Queen Street,
Maidenhead, Berkshire, from stories first published in
Brownie Annuals 1970, 1971, 1972, 1973, 1974, 1975, 1976, 1977
Made and printed in Great Britain by Purnell and Sons Limited,
Paulton (Bristol) and London

CONTENTS

SIXTEEN OF THE BEST

The sixteen delightful stories in this book have been specially selected from the many published in the *Brownie Annual*.

They will nearly all be new to you, and, Brownies, you will love them! So will your Guiders, who will find them just right for telling to their Packs at meetings or on Pack holidays.

One or two of the stories take you abroad, and you will thoroughly enjoy the adventures of Bulbuls in India and Brownie Guides in Nigeria.

There are thrills, excitement and surprises in plenty, but there are touching incidents too that may bring a tear or two to your eyes.

Beautifully illustrated, this is a book you will read, enjoy, and treasure.

Robert Moss

Editor of the Brownie Annual

A Present From Julie

by NORA BLAZE

"Good King Wenceslas looked out," sang the Brownies, "on the feast of Stephen, when the snow lay round about, deep and crisp and even."

Julie sang as joyfully as anyone. She had only become a Brownie a few months ago and she loved every minute of Pack meetings, and all the activities. Now they were practising carols. On Christmas morning they were all going to the children's ward of the hospital to sing to the small patients, and Julie was looking forward to this eagerly.

When they had gone through the three carols they were practising, the Brownie Guider said it was time for Pow-wow.

"Now, Brownies," she began, when they were all sitting in the Pow-wow Ring, "you older ones will know that besides singing for the children every Christmas we give them presents as well—or, rather, we collect all we can and hand them in to the hospital just before Christmas."

Julie listened with interest. She would ask her mother to buy something really special for her to give.

"Of course," went on the Guider, as though she had read Julie's thoughts, "you don't *buy* the presents. You give whatever you can spare from your own toys; nothing broken or dirty, of course. We shouldn't like anyone to give *us* anything like that, should we? I know most of you take care of your things, so I'm sure there is just one book or toy you can spare, but it must be nice and clean. We have always had a splendid collection in other years, so let's see what we can do this time, and think how grateful we shall be that we are not spending Christmas in hospital!"

Julie walked home thoughtfully. What on earth could she give? Her parents always gave her expensive presents—she knew that this Christmas she was having a bicycle—and she didn't want to give any of them away.

"Couldn't you buy a toy for me to give, Mummy?" she asked when she got home. "Brown Owl would never know!"

"Oh, no, dear!" her mother said. "That would be like telling an untruth, wouldn't it? We can't do that! There must be something you have finished playing with that you could give."

Julie thought. "Oh, I know!" she exclaimed. "They can have that big jigsaw puzzle of Windsor Castle."

Her mother shook her head and said no. Julie had forgotten; one of the pieces was lost. Besides, how could a girl or boy put a jigsaw together in bed? A big flat table would be needed, so that was no good.

"One of your books perhaps?" Mummy suggested. "You've got heaps of nice books."

"But I *want* all my books!" said Julie crossly. "I like them, and I don't want to part with any of them."

Her mother sighed. She had thought several times lately that Julie was becoming a rather selfish girl, perhaps because she had no sisters or brothers. She was pleased when Julie joined the Brownies, hoping they would teach her to think more of others and less of herself. She remembered the days when she herself had been a Brownie and then a Guide.

It was when she was kissing Julie goodnight that she noticed the big teddy bear sitting up against the wall on the chest of drawers.

"Why, Julie, you can give them that old teddy bear! You haven't played with him for years."

"Oh, no, Mummy!" cried Julie, in dismay. "Not Teddy! I simply can't give them Teddy!"

"Why ever not?" Her mother lifted the teddy bear down. "Look at him, just sitting here doing nothing but collecting dust. You can't possibly want to keep him."

"Yes, I do," said Julie sulkily. "And, anyway, Brown Owl said they must be clean things."

"I'll soon make him clean!" her mother said cheerfully. "He's the kind you can put in a washing-machine and see come out just like new!"

"But I don't *want* to give him away!" shouted Julie, in tears.

"Julie, dear," her mother said gently, sitting down on the bed, "you know quite well you don't really want him any more. I don't believe you've even noticed him for a long time. When you get your bicycle you won't want your dolls, either."

"They're not having any of my dolls," muttered Julie sullenly.

"Well, never mind," her mother said, kissing her again and getting up to go. "Go to sleep now and in the morning perhaps we can think of something else." She closed the bedroom door quietly and went downstairs.

By the light of the street lamp outside Julie could see Teddy sitting where her mother had replaced him. He'd always sat there, she thought mutinously. Why should she give him away?

When she woke the next morning she found it had snowed hard in the night. As it was Saturday, she would be able to play with her sledge or something. She washed and dressed quickly and ran downstairs, her usual happy self.

At ten o'clock her mother went out of the front gate, basket on arm, to go to the shops, but when she saw what Julie was doing she became very cross.

"Julie," she exclaimed, "stop that at once! I've told you before not to make a slide on the pavement. If anyone slipped on it they might break an arm or leg."

"Oh, bother!" said Julie. She had been enjoying herself sliding up and down. Grown-ups were always spoiling your fun!

"I can't bear to part with him!"

"Go in and get the bag of cooking salt from the kitchen and sprinkle it all over the slide. Really, Julie, you are old enough now to give a little thought to other people! Remember your Brownie Law!"

Mummy walked on, carefully avoiding the ice, and Julie, muttering to herself, fetched the salt and threw it over her lovely slide. The ice crackled and melted, and soon, instead of the dangerous slide, there was a clear length of pavement where anyone could walk safely.

When she took the salt back Julie saw a stiff broom. Taking it outside, she swept all the pavement in front of the house clear of snow, which she pushed into the gutter. When her mother returned she was delighted.

"That's a much more sensible thing to do! I wish everyone would clear their piece of pavement. I nearly fell down on one of the worst bits."

After that, Julie felt she simply had to sweep the stretch in front of the old lady's next door. "And that's my good turn for today," she told herself, feeling warm all over.

It was soon Monday again. When Julie got home from school, there was Teddy on the kitchen table, all clean and fluffy, having been in the washing-machine and spin-drier that morning.

Julie snatched him up and hugged him.

"Oh, Mummy! He looks just like new! I can't bear to part with him!"

"Well, please yourself," said her mother resignedly. "But you'll have to find something before Friday. That's when you all have to take the presents, isn't it?"

"Yes," answered Julie absently. She was remembering when Teddy had been really new. What a little girl she was then, only about two! Perhaps she *was* too old for a teddy bear now. But he was so cuddly! She took him up to her room, sat him on the chest of drawers again, and touched his golden fur gently with her fingers. She looked round her pretty bedroom and saw her dolls: Esmeralda, who walked and talked; Mandy, whose hair could be washed and reset; Cindy, the teenage-doll with several changes of clothes; and the baby who drank from a bottle and then had to have her nappy changed! She looked at her doll's pram and cot, complete with pillows, sheets and covers. Then she looked at her row of books, exciting adventure stories that she often read again, big annuals, and books with beautiful pictures in them. Then she looked back at Teddy. His round brown eyes seemed to be watching her. Did she imagine a look of reproach in them?

After tea on Friday, when she had put on her Brownie uniform, she picked the bear up and held him against her for a minute. Tears pricked her eyes. Then resolutely tucking him under one arm, she ran downstairs and asked if she could have some tissue-paper.

Her mother looked up in surprise; then a pleased smile came over her face.

"You're going to give your teddy to the hospital? I *am* glad. I know you won't regret it. I've some nice new tissue-paper you can have to wrap him in." And she went to fetch it.

All the way to the Church institute Julie held the bear close. When the Brownies were all handing in their presents she held him out silently, knowing that if she said anything she would cry. The Guider thanked her and carefully unwrapped the paper.

"Oh, Julie, how kind of you! What a beautiful teddy bear! Are you sure——?" Then she caught sight of Julie's tremulous smile and wisely said no more.

That night Julie cried into her pillow. It seemed so lonely without Teddy sitting there, and she thought of him going to live with another girl, who couldn't possibly love him as she had.

Christmas Day came, a sunny, frosty day, and the Brownies assembled at the hospital gate before going in to the children's ward to sing carols. The long ward was gaily decorated with paper chains and balloons, with a big Christmas tree in the middle from which the presents had been distributed earlier.

After the carols, the Brownies dispersed about the ward to talk to the patients. Julie found herself near a bed where a small girl lay fast asleep. In her arms was—Julie caught her breath—yes, it was dear old Teddy! The child's thin little arms were clasped tightly around him. Her cheek lay against his furry head, and on her pale face was a look of complete bliss. Her left leg was encased in a thick white plaster cast, held up by a rope fastened to a pulley.

A big lump came into Julie's throat as she stood there looking down. A nurse, passing, stopped and said quietly, "That's little Jill. She's only three and a half. She slipped on the ice and broke her leg in two places. She'll be here for weeks, and since she was brought in she's done nothing but cry—until this morning, when we gave her that beautiful teddy some kind person sent. You ought to have seen her face! She stopped crying right away, and this is the first real sleep she's had since her accident. I wish we knew whom to thank."

Julie was just going to say "It was me" when the nurse hurried away; and then she was glad she hadn't said it. Her reward was in seeing Teddy in those loving little arms. He would keep Jill company in hospital and for long afterwards.

As Julie ran home she was glad—very glad—that she had given Teddy away.

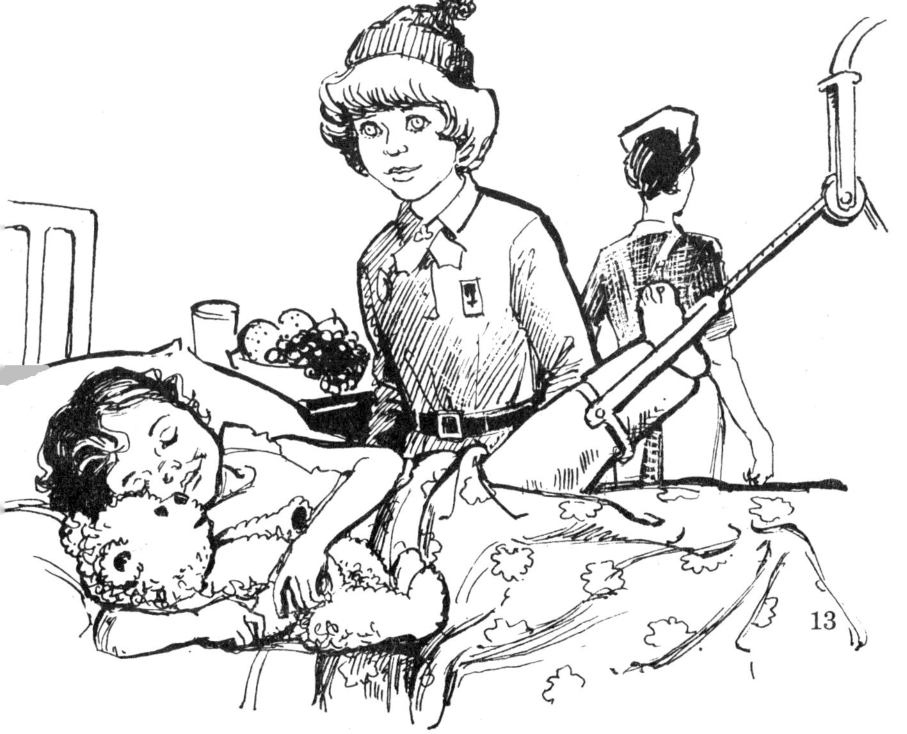

The Mystery of the Christmas Pudding

by EDNA GILBERT

It was, without a doubt, the most gorgeous Christmas pudding the Brownies had ever seen!

Now out of its white basin, neatly arranged on a lace doily and with a sprig of red-berried holly as decoration, it stood proudly on a long table laden with an assortment of gaily wrapped gifts, every one of which had been painstakingly made by Brownies in the Pack. It wasn't just the appearance of the pudding which drew excited comments from everyone present, but the delicious aroma of nutmeg and spices which hung around it, causing mouths to water and tongues to wag!

"Did you make it yourself?" asked Joy of her friend, Amanda.

She knew, of course, as the Brownies knew, that Amanda liked home-making and that she always helped her mother with the housework; but she had never given them any idea that she was a good cook too! Why, she didn't even have her Cook badge yet!

Joy could have bitten her tongue the moment she had spoken. She knew Amanda. Amanda was her best friend . . . and she didn't cheat!

Two months before, on a golden October evening, their Brownie Guider had asked them to form a Pow-wow Ring.

"Time for a very special Pow-wow," she said, as they gathered round. "As you all know," she went on, "this will be our first Christmas since we have been holding our meetings at the 'Hollies', thanks to Miss Plunkett. We have had many happy hours here, and I am sure you will all want to show your appreciation. I think it would be a nice gesture if every one of us made a small gift, either for Miss Plunkett or for her companion, Martha. It need not be expensive—a hand-painted Christmas card, a drawing, an embroidered handkerchief—but whatever the choice make it yourself—don't buy it. Please keep this a secret from Miss Plunkett. We want this to be a very special surprise for her!"

Now, at last, it was only a few days before Christmas. The two Brownie Guiders, Mrs. Long and Georgina, had worked hard decorating the "workroom" with holly and mistletoe. The gifts the Brownies had made were of all shapes and sizes, and all were neatly wrapped, with the exception of the pudding. It was hardly surprising, when Miss Plunkett arrived, that this should be the first thing that caught her eye.

"Oh," she cried, clasping her hands together as a child does when excited, "what a beautiful Christmas pudding!"

Mrs. Long stepped forward. "It's for you, dear Miss Plunkett," she said. "Every gift here is either for you or Martha. The Brownies have made them because they love you, and are grateful to you for letting us use your lovely home for our meetings."

For a moment there wasn't a sound in the workroom. Then Miss Plunkett, dabbing her eyes with a wisp of lace handkerchief but smiling through her tears, whispered, "Thank you all very much!"

One by one the presents were unwrapped. Every Brownie was praised and thanked in turn, and everyone was in the very gayest of Christmas spirits.

"Martha and I," announced Miss Plunkett, "will have the pudding for our Christmas dinner. Really, Amanda, I never knew you were such a clever cook!"

It was then that an odd thing happened. As soon as Miss Plunkett had spoken, Amanda flushed and looked as if she were about to say something. Only Mrs. Long noticed, and she, who knew every one of her Brownies well, wondered suddenly if Amanda was hiding a small secret.

"Maybe," thought Mrs. Long, "her mother did most of the cooking."

It was understandable that Amanda's mother should help her. After all, most first tries into cooking were done with someone's help. There was really no need for Amanda to feel guilty about it. All the same, it was strange Amanda hadn't mentioned that her mother had helped her.

At the first Pack meeting after Christmas the Brownies had a surprise. They had all received Venture badges for taking part in making gifts for Miss Plunkett.

"Amanda is the first to have passed the Cooking Challenge on the Brownie Highway," said Mrs. Long. "Miss Plunkett and Martha say hers was the most delicious pudding they've ever tasted!"

All the Brownies clapped their hands and looked at Amanda, who sat quite still. Then, to everyone's horror, she suddenly stood up, burst into tears, and said, "Oh, no, it's no use; it wouldn't be right!" and without another word she ran out of the room.

Whatever had happened to Amanda? What was wrong to make her say it wouldn't be right for her to be passed for her Cooking Challenge? Why was she crying? The Brownies didn't know what to make of it all, but Mrs. Long had a shrewd idea. Hastily, after sending the Brownies to their Six homes, she went out in search of Amanda.

She didn't have to go far. Curled up on one of the big circular window-seats in the concert room, Amanda was sobbing as if her heart would break. She didn't stop when Mrs. Long gently took out her own handkerchief to wipe the tears away.

"Was it that you didn't really make the pudding, Amanda?" Mrs. Long asked softly. "It doesn't matter, you know, if your mummy helped. Please tell me about it!"

Amanda stopped crying abruptly. Her eyes, streaked with tears, were wide open in hurt anger.

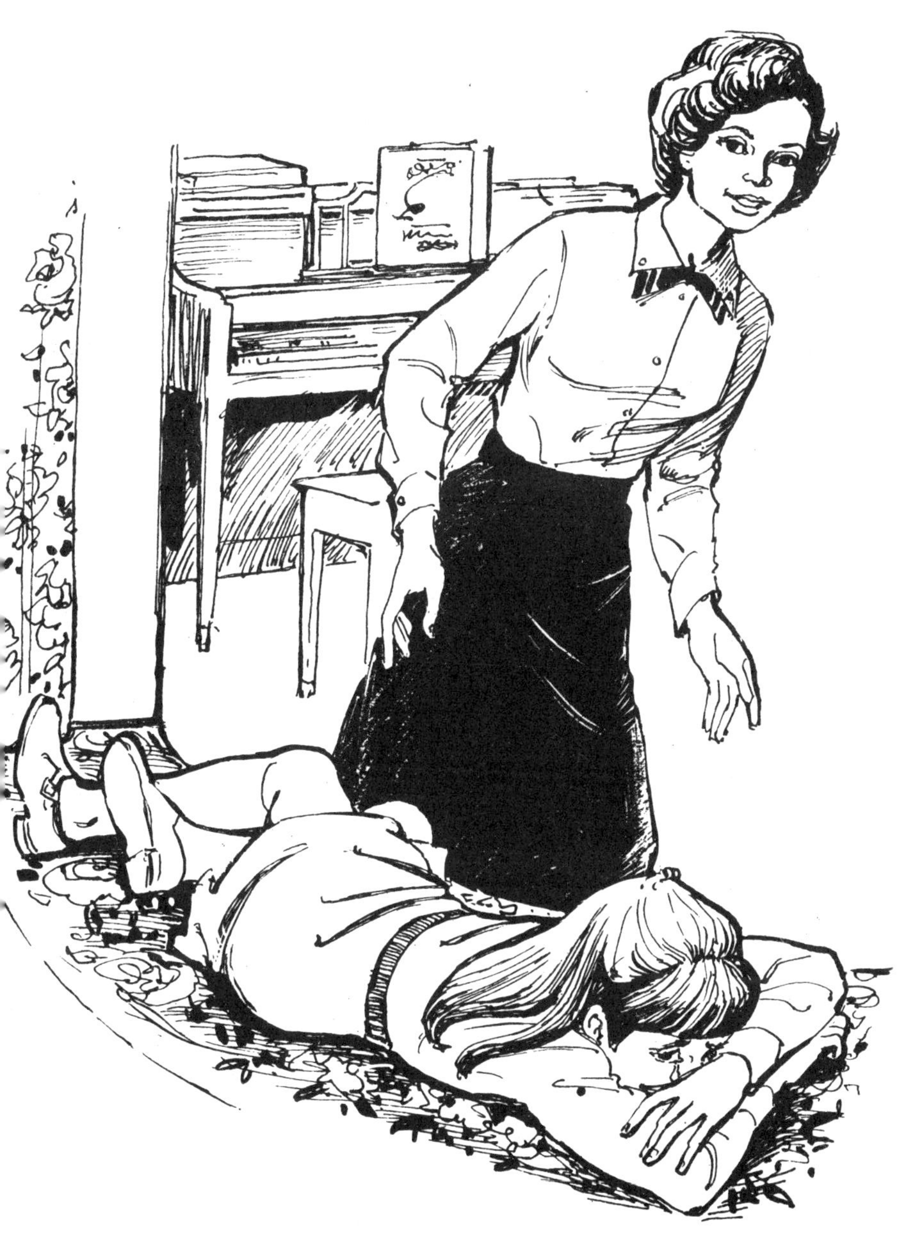

Amanda sobbed as if her heart would break

"Nobody helped me!" she cried. "I did it all myself. I weighed every ounce, followed every rule, baked it at the exact heat. The only thing is——" and here, once again, her voice choked with her emotion. "The only thing is," she repeated, "it should have been a CAKE!"

It was no use! Mrs. Long had to laugh. She knew she shouldn't have done so, but this was one explanation she had never dreamed of! At first, Amanda watched her unbelievingly; then slowly a smile spread over her own face. In a minute they were both laughing together, the tears, this time of mirth, spilling down their faces!

"So what went wrong?" asked Mrs. Long, recovering her composure but still dabbing her eyes with the sodden handkerchief they were now sharing.

"I lifted it carefully out of the tin," Amanda told her, "and it wobbled! It was still wobbling next morning, and again at teatime. I didn't know what to do. Whoever heard of a wobbly Christmas cake? I lay awake all night, and next morning I heard Mum say she had bought a Christmas pudding! It was then that I had a great idea!"

"Yes?" prompted Mrs. Long.

"I put the whole lot into a basin," said Amanda, "and boiled it!"

Well, Amanda passed her Cooking Challenge. All the Brownies and Mrs. Long and Miss Plunkett agreed that she deserved it. She had shown imagination and originality.

"Anyone else," said Miss Plunkett, "might have thrown the cake to the birds, and then Martha and I would not have had such a wonderful Christmas dinner! Amanda, you must give Martha the recipe!"

Amanda's eyes twinkled. "For the cake, do you mean, Miss Plunkett?"

"Indeed not!" laughed Miss Plunkett. "For the pudding, of course!"

A Present From the Pack

by MARGARET HINCHLIFFE

Linda Worthington pulled her Brownie beret on to her fair hair, then peeped out of her bedroom window to see if her friend, Ann Walton, was coming. Yes, there she was, walking jauntily down the road, wearing her Brownie uniform.

Linda ran down the stairs. "Bye, Mummy!" she called out to her mother, who was in the kitchen. "I'm going to Brownies now."

"Goodbye, dear! Try not to let Patch follow you this time."

Linda met her friend at the gate. Ann was bubbling over with news, and couldn't wait to tell Linda what she had just heard.

"Guess what, Linda!" she cried. "Tawny Owl has a secret to tell us, and it's something to do with Brown Owl. I saw Tawny on my way from school today, and she told me to tell as many Brownies as possible that she wants to get us all together sometime when Brown Owl isn't there."

Linda's eyes grew wide. "Whatever can it be!" she asked.

"I don't know," replied Ann, "but let's hurry; then we might find out tonight."

The Guide and Scout headquarters was only a few minutes' walk down the road from Linda's home. Just as the two girls were about to turn in at the gate, they heard a familiar sound behind them. It was the patter of a dog's paws.

"Patch, you naughty dog, go home!" scolded Linda. "You're always following me to Pack meeting. You mustn't! You aren't a Brownie, you know. Go home at once."

Linda tried to sound stern, but the brown-and-white spaniel, who was little more than a puppy, just stood wagging his tail and gazing up pleadingly at his mistress with his soft brown eyes.

Linda relented and chuckled. "All right, you win! You can just peep in, then off you go home."

Patch trotted up behind the girls and into the hall. He scampered round the room and barked, as much as to say, "Hello, Brownies!" Then, at Linda's command, he trotted obediently home.

Everyone was present except the Brownie Guider, Miss Lucy. The Assistant Guider, Lorraine, looked pleased as she gave the silence signal.

"Brown Owl isn't coming tonight, Pack," she told them. "She has some very important things to do, so this is an excellent opportunity for me to let you into a secret."

The Brownies looked at each other expectantly.

"First of all," Lorraine went on, "Brown Owl is getting married soon. I'm sorry to say we shall be losing her. She is going to live several miles away from here."

There were cries of disappointment then, for the Brownies were all fond of their pretty Guider.

"But," continued Lorraine, "I want you to think about what we can give her for a wedding present. I thought it would be nice to give her a tablecloth with all our names embroidered on it. We can each embroider our own name, then we shall each have contributed something. It can be our new Pack Venture; but we must keep it a secret from Brown Owl."

There was a chorus of agreement. Only one Brownie felt a little worried about the present. It was Linda.

"I'm sure to make a mess of my part," she thought. "If I prick my finger, as I usually do, I might get blood on the tablecloth. If only my name wasn't so long—Linda Worthington! I ask you! It'll take me simply ages to do."

Linda wasn't a very good sewer, but she did intend to work for her Needleworker badge as a Challenge. When it came to embroidering a wedding present, though, she didn't feel very capable. She was afraid she might spoil it.

When Lorraine told them that the fairest way would be for each Brownie to take her turn in alphabetical order of surnames, Linda cheered up.

"Good! I'm W, so that means I shall be last," she thought. "That'll give me time to practise."

The Brownie Guider was absent the following week, too. Lorraine brought out of her shopping-bag a tablecloth in a pretty shade of yellow. She spread it out on a table. In the centre, in brown embroidery thread, she had worked the Brownie Promise badge and the words SECOND WESTBRIDGE PACK. It made an attractive design. In each corner she had embroidered in the same colour, SPRITES, ELVES, PIXIES and GNOMES.

"Each Six can sign their names in the appropriate corner. Elves, you begin." She handed a pencil to the Sixer of the Elves and showed her where to sign her name.

At last all the names were signed, under Lorraine's supervision. Next she wrote out a list of names so that each Brownie knew to whom she must pass the tablecloth.

Lorraine told them to work the names in chain-stitch, and Linda practised hard on scraps of material. She improved slowly, but still continued to prick her finger.

"I wish, now, that my name came near the beginning of the alphabet, then I would have done my share!" she thought, unhappily.

But she need not have worried, for when her turn came, one Saturday, she embroidered her name in the Sprites' corner, just as nicely as the rest. There was only one speck of blood, which she managed to cover with embroidery.

She spread the tablecloth out on the floor. It really was very nice.

"I hope Brown Owl likes it," Linda remarked to her mother, who was arranging flowers at the sideboard.

"Oh, Patch—you naughty, naughty dog!"

Mrs. Worthington turned to admire the cloth. "I'm sure she will," she said. "It's lovely."

"Tawny asked me to take it round to her house as soon as I had finished," Linda said, "so I'll go tonight, after tea. She wants to wash it, because it is a bit grubby now, isn't it? We're giving it to Brown Owl next week. She's getting married in a fortnight, you know."

Just then Daddy came in with Patch. They had had a lovely walk. But a terrible thing happened. In his eagerness to greet the rest of the family, Patch walked over the precious tablecloth, leaving dirty paw-prints on it.

Linda let out a loud wail. "Oh, Patch—you naughty, naughty dog!"

There was no consoling Linda then. She sobbed and sobbed, tears rolling down her cheeks.

"Oh, whatever is Tawny going to say?" she cried. "I never thought something like this would happen."

"I think it will wash out, dear," comforted Mummy. "You can't really blame Patch, you know. He wasn't to know. Why not take the tablecloth round to Tawny Owl after tea and tell her what happened."

Linda nodded and dried her tears.

All the same, it was a very nervous Brownie who knocked on Lorraine's door that evening.

Haltingly she explained what had happened. Lorraine looked dismayed when she saw the tablecloth, and Linda could hardly stop tears flowing.

Suddenly Lorraine smiled. "Never mind, Linda! It will be all right. Don't worry any more about it."

"Are you sure?" asked Linda uncertainly.

"Quite sure," replied Lorraine. "I'm going to wash it; then it will be as good as new."

Linda left Lorraine's feeling a little happier.

The next Brownie meeting was a sad as well as a happy event. It was their Guider's last evening with them.

Lorraine had packed the tablecloth in a nice box and wrapped this

Lorraine was smiling across at her

in silvery wedding paper. It looked most attractive.

Linda thought that the tablecloth must be all right, or she felt sure Lorraine would have mentioned it.

When the Guider opened the box and unfolded the tablecloth, tears came into her eyes.

"How lovely!" she said. "A tablecloth with all your names beautifully embroidered on it, and—yes—even Patch's paw-marks! You couldn't very well leave him out, could you—he's such a regular visitor! He's certainly one of us now. I shall always remember the Second Westbridge Pack. Thank you very, very much."

Linda sat bolt upright as she stared at the tablecloth, which the Guider held up. Yes, there were Patch's paw-marks for everyone to see, but cleverly embroidered in brown silk!

Linda glanced at Lorraine, who was smiling across at her. Lorraine winked her eye, as much as to say, "I told you it would be all right, didn't I?"

Linda grinned back.

"Good old Patch!" she thought. "I'm glad you put your paw-marks on the present. It makes it complete, somehow!"

The Special Good Turn

by R. E. PLAISTED

The Brownies were all working in their Six homes when Brown Owl called to Ann.

"Did you know that you have only one more test to pass to earn your Discoverer Badge, Ann?" she asked. "You've only got to find your way to an unknown spot by compass and other directions."

Ann nodded, but looked glum. "I know, Brown Owl, but I'm scared of it. I'm sure I couldn't find my way anywhere if I didn't know the path or road or anything."

"You've learned about the compass, and you've got sharp eyes. What you need to do now is to learn to use those eyes. As next week is a school holiday," went on Brown Owl, "it will be a good opportunity for you to put in some practice at keeping your eyes wide open to notice things."

"I'll try, Brown Owl," said Ann doubtfully.

"Good!" Brown Owl said. "I think we'll have a game now."

After the game, Brown Owl called the Pack into a Pow-wow circle. The Brownies sat down, chattering noisily about the coming holiday.

"I'm going to the seaside," said Susan.

"I'm staying at home, but Mummy's promised to take us out most days."

"I've got to mind my little sister."

Brown Owl raised her hand and waited. The chattering gradually ceased as each Brownie also raised her hand. When there was complete silence, all the hands were lowered and Brown Owl began to speak.

"Next week there will be no Pack Meeting," she said, and paused, waiting for the groans to stop. "Some of you are going away on holiday, as I shall be, but I want you all to remember that you are Brownies. Can any of you think of a way to be specially helpful this week?"

Linda raised her hand. "I could help my mummy with the baby," she said.

"Help pack clothes and things," suggested Susan.

"Make the beds," said Fiona.

Brown Owl smiled."Those are all good ideas, but I want each Brownie to try to do a special good turn during this next week when you are all on holiday. I'm sure you can all think of something. Will you all try?"

The Brownies nodded.

After Pack Meeting Ann walked home with her friend, Linda.

"What are you going to do for your special good turn, Ann?" asked Linda.

"I don't think I'll tell you," Ann replied. "I'd rather keep it secret."

Ann really had no idea what to do for a special good turn, but she did not want to admit it, even to Linda.

The next day was very hot, and Ann decided to go to the woods during the afternoon to look for leaves, of which she was making a collection.

"I wonder whether I could do my special good turn this morning," she thought; but try as she would she couldn't think of a good turn that would be in any way special. She had washed the dishes, made her bed, and gone shopping for her mother, but these were everyday good turns that couldn't really count as being "special".

Ann set out for the woods, taking one of her mother's shopping baskets to put the leaves into. The woods were not far away, and

Suddenly Ann saw a small girl under a tree

before long Ann's feet were sinking into the grass and leaves beneath the trees. She strolled along happily, looking for unusual leaves and placing them when she found them carefully in the basket. She forgot the time as she went from tree to tree.

It must have been an hour later that she began to feel vaguely uneasy. The heat had become oppressive, and the woods were strangely silent. Not a leaf stirred; even the birds had ceased singing.

"I believe there's a storm brewing," Ann said to herself. "I'd better get home quickly before the rain starts."

She turned and began to run along the footpath towards home. Suddenly she heard a faint cry. Pausing, she held her breath and listened. There it was again! Whoever had called sounded very frightened.

Just at that moment a flash of lightning lit up the woods. This was followed by a deafening roll of thunder.

Ann was terrified of thunderstorms. She began to run on again, but then suddenly stopped. The cry had come again, but louder this time and, Ann thought, even more frightened.

"I must go and see who it is," she decided, and turned in the direction from which the cry had come.

A flash of lightning lit the woods again, and thunder crashed menacingly. Then heavy rain began to fall.

"There's no need to be scared, really," Ann told herself bravely, but she *was* scared! She remembered hearing about people being struck by lightning while sheltering under a tree. She began to imagine herself trapped under a fallen tree, but then she shook her head and thrust the horrible picture out of her mind.

The cry came again, quite close, and suddenly Ann saw a small girl crouched under a tree. The child was clutching a bedraggled puppy, which was whimpering and trying to lick the tears that rolled down the toddler's face.

Ann ran up to the forlorn child. "What's the matter?" she asked. "Are you lost?"

The child, who could not have been more than two or three years old, looked up at Ann through tear-stained eyes and then began crying again. The puppy growled at Ann, then sneezed softly.

Ann laughed, in spite of her fears.

"What's your name," she asked.

"Pat," the child mumbled.

"Where do you live, Pat?"

"Don't know." She began to cry harder.

Lightning struck again across the woods. It was followed by the crashing of a falling tree.

Ann shuddered. The noise of the falling tree and the roar of the thunder were more terrifying to her than to the child, but she fought off the panic that threatened to grip her.

"Where do you live?" she asked the little girl again. "What are you doing in the woods all by yourself? Where is your mummy?"

"Don't know. Pat lost."

Ann felt in her pockets and found the sweet she knew was there.

"Here you are, Pat."

Pat took the sweet and sucked it. Her sobs became quieter and gradually died away. Ann stroked the puppy.

"Which way is home, puppy?" she asked, but the little dog only wagged its tail and licked Ann's face.

Again the thunder bellowed, but this time Ann ignored it.

"Try to remember which way you came," she said to Pat.

Pat looked up, but said nothing. Ann felt rather desperate. There were half a dozen paths through the woods. Pat was too young to have wandered very far, Ann reasoned, so she probably came from one of the cottages on the edge of the woods; but they might walk for miles in the wrong direction if they didn't take the right path.

Suddenly Ann remembered the Discoverer Badge. In the test she would have to find her way to an unknown spot, keeping her eyes wide open to notice things that would lead her in the right direction. She had dreaded this last test for the badge, but Brown Owl had said she had sharp eyes and only needed to use them. She suddenly realised that Pat would be sure to have left some signs of her passage through the woods. If she could find just one it would put her on the right track homeward.

"Pat," she said, "you must show me the way you came."

Pat looked blank.

"We must find your mummy, Pat. Is your house this way?" Ann walked away, but the child took no notice. Then Ann suddenly saw a small handkerchief lying beside one of the paths.

"Mine!" Pat nodded as Ann held it up. Ann breathed a sigh of relief. If the handkerchief really was Pat's, they had at least made a start in finding the way home.

"Come along, Pat; I'll take you home," Ann said, and waited while the child toddled up to her with the puppy.

Slowly they began the walk along the path, the puppy weaving happily between their legs, until another loud roll of thunder had him whimpering in terror. Ann picked him up and snuggled him against her.

"It's lucky Pat isn't scared of thunder," Ann thought. "She would be too heavy for me to cuddle or carry."

As they made their way beneath the dripping branches, Ann looked for more signs that would assure her they were on the right path. She noticed broken twigs and downtrodden grass, which showed that someone had been that way, but whether it was Pat or someone else Ann could not tell. Presently, however, she noticed several dying flowers alongside the path, and a sudden thought struck her.

"Were you picking flowers, Pat?" she asked.

Pat nodded, and Ann felt sure now that she was on the right path.

Suddenly the puppy wriggled, jumped from Ann's arms, and ran off. He began digging frantically under a tree and returned with a bone in his mouth, his tail wagging madly.

Ann sighed with relief. "That means they came this way," she said to herself. "Perhaps their house is close now. Oh, I do hope so! We seem to have been walking for hours."

Both Ann and the child were soaking wet. Pat began to cry again. She asked to be carried.

Suddenly a woman appeared among the trees.

Pat recognised her mother at once

"Pat, is that you?" she cried.

Pat recognised her mother at once, broke away from Ann, and scurried along the path.

"Where have you been, you naughty girl?" Pat's mother scolded.

Ann ran along the path. "I found her crying in the woods," she said. "I don't know how she got there."

"Come along to the cottage and dry yourself," Pat's mother invited.

The cottage was not far away. Ann was thankful to see it. As Pat's mother opened the door, Ann saw that a fire was burning in the grate, and smelt warm bread.

Both girls were quickly relieved of their wet clothes and then wrapped in blankets. Soon they were sitting before the fire with mugs of hot cocoa.

Pat's mother came and sat down beside them.

"I've found out how Pat came to wander off," she told Ann. "The fence is broken, and she must have squeezed through the gap. Where do you live, Ann?"

"In Leaf Lane," Ann told her.

"Are you on the telephone?"

"Yes," Ann replied.

"If you will tell me your number I'll ring up your parents and let them know that you are safe."

Ann gave her the information, and she left the cottage to telephone. She came back about fifteen minutes later.

"You can stay to tea, Ann, if you would like to, and your father will fetch you when he comes home from work."

It was several hours later, when Ann was safely back at home, that she remembered the leaves she had collected.

"I must have left the basket in the woods," she thought. "I'll go back tomorrow for it."

She found the basket the next morning, but the leaves were ruined.

"Never mind," she said. "I can easily collect some more."

During the remainder of the week, Ann pressed the leaves,

Wrapped in blankets they drank hot cocoa

mounted them, looked up their names in a book she borrowed from the public library, then carefully printed the name beside each leaf.

At the next Pack meeting, Brown Owl asked whether the Brownies had all remembered to do a special good turn. Some Brownies had, some hadn't; some shuffled their feet, and some said and did nothing at all. Then Brown Owl took a letter from her pocket and read it out. It was from Pat's mother, and had been passed on to Brown Owl by Ann's mother, who hadn't told Ann about it. It thanked and praised Ann for looking after Pat and for so cleverly finding her way home.

"It just shows you what you can do if you really try," Brown Owl said. "Finding the way was the part of the Discoverer Badge test you really dreaded, wasn't it, Ann? Well, you proved that you could do it by being alert and using your eyes, even under very difficult conditions. You can certainly count what you did for Pat and her mother as a special good turn—don't you think so, Brownies?"

All the Brownies nodded or shouted "yes" with great vigour.

"You'll still have to pass the test with a tester, Ann," went on Brown Owl, "but I'm quite sure now that you'll pass."

A week or so later, Ann took the final part of the test for the Discoverer Badge. She did so with a confidence she wouldn't have dreamed she possessed a week earlier, and was praised by the tester for the keen way she found signs and landmarks that would guide her along the right path.

Now she not only wears the Discoverer Badge and the Collector Badge, but under her Six Emblem is a Second stripe!

The Surprise Prize

by G. EVANSON

Jane and Susan were exactly the same age. They lived next door to each other; they went to the same school, and they had joined the local Brownie Guide Pack at the same time. They were great friends.

At one Pack meeting in late summer the Brownie Guider announced an exciting competition. The Guider was named Miss Penn, and the Brownies had voted to call her, instead of Brown Owl, "Penny".

"I'm going to give a prize for the best bowl of daffodils grown by one of you by the spring," said Penny, who was very fond of flowers. "I will show you what to do. If you will each bring a bowl, some bulb fibre and six daffodil bulbs to our next Pack meeting we will plant them."

Jane and Susan each took bowls and shared a bag of fibre. They had six bulbs each, as Penny had suggested.

Penny was pleased that all the Brownies remembered to bring the things she had asked for. She showed them how to put the bulbs in the fibre and watched to see that they planted them so that the sharp green shoots would appear at the top.

When all the bulbs were planted, she said: "It is best to put them outside for about six weeks covered with straw. Make sure that mice can't get at them or they'll nibble them. In October take them indoors. Keep them in a dark place till green shoots appear. Then they can stand in the light, though not in too warm a room."

All the Brownies took care to do as Penny had told them. During the winter months, at Pack meetings, they asked each other how the bulbs were coming on. Jane and Susan hoped that theirs would be the best daffodils. They were thrilled when buds began to show among the long leaves.

A few days before the Pack meeting at which the daffodils were to be judged by Penny, Susan fell ill. She was not able to go to the meeting, and was bitterly disappointed.

"Never mind!" said Jane, trying to cheer her friend up. "I'll take your bowl for you."

Jane could see that Susan's daffodils were growing well, but she knew that her own were much better. She hadn't seen the other Brownies' flowers, but her own looked really lovely, and she thought she stood a very good chance of winning Penny's prize.

She felt very sorry that Susan wasn't able to be at the meeting and see all the entries. Then suddenly an idea flashed into her mind.

"If I don't take my bowl Susan's may have a chance of winning!"

So, without a word to anyone, Jane took Susan's bowl of daffodils along to the meeting, leaving her own at home.

Penny inspected each Brownie's plants closely and carefully and then said: "I have decided to award the prize to Susan. No one else has as many blooms, and although one or two of Susan's are too tall I am sure hers deserve the prize."

Jane was delighted, and at the end of the meeting hurried to Susan's house to give her Penny's prize of a set of small garden tools.

Susan's pleasure at winning more than made up for Jane's sacrifice of her own entry.

Next day Penny called to see how Susan was and to congratulate her on winning the prize. Afterwards she called on Jane's mummy. In the house she noticed a bowl of daffodils.

"Did you grow those, Mrs. Graham?" she asked admiringly.

"I'll take your bowl for you"

Mrs. Graham suddenly realised that Jane hadn't said anything more about her daffodils, and when Penny told her that the Brownies' plants had been judged the previous evening and that Susan's had won the prize, she realised that Jane had deliberately not taken her entry to the meeting.

"I think I can guess why," she said quietly.

"So can I," said Penny. "Jane is a very unselfish girl. We mustn't let Susan know or it might spoil her pleasure at winning. If I hadn't happened to call on you we'd never have known what Jane did."

The next day the postman brought a parcel for Jane.

"Whatever can this be?" cried Jane. "It isn't my birthday."

Opening the parcel, she saw that it contained a set of small garden tools, just like those given to Susan as her prize. Inside was a note from Penny, which said: *I have decided to give two prizes instead of one, and this is yours, Jane.*

The Unexpected Pet

by JOYCE STRANGER

Odette stood against the wall of the Guide hall for a moment, watching the other Brownies enjoying themselves. Next week they would be meeting as usual, and she would be stuck in a mouldy caravan in the wildest part of Scotland.

"Come on, Odette," the Brownie Guider said. "It's not the end of the world."

"I wish Daddy had a different job or at least could go without us," Odette said angrily.

"It's a fascinating job," said the Brownie Guider. And you wouldn't really like to be without him for a year while he was away building a bridge, would you?"

Odette wanted nothing better than to live in a house in the same town for the rest of her life, as other girls did. Instead, she had been born in Brazil, spent four years in Spain and three in France, and the rest of her life had been made up of a year here and two years there, in various parts of the British Isles.

She remembered the words a week later as she finished the day's work and sat down to tea. The caravan had been placed beside a loch, and the sun glimmered red on the high peaks, which showed a constantly shifting pattern of light and dark.

"It's beautiful here," her mother said.

Odette would much rather have been with the rest of the Brownies, having fun in the Guide hall.

"Why don't you write to the Pack?" her mother suggested. "I'm sure they'd all be interested in hearing from you."

"There's nothing to write about," said Odette.

Her mother did not persist. Privately, she felt sorry for Odette and sometimes wondered if it would not be kinder to send her to a boarding-school, but both her parents felt that the experience of travelling all over the world gave Odette something to make up for the lack of company.

Winter came. One evening, when frost had the whole of the loch and the river by the throat, Odette felt she could not endure the cramped caravan one moment longer. She put on stout shoes, scarf and thick coat, and took a torch.

The field they were in was rough grass, and a couple of cows looked at her curiously as she passed. She walked towards the stream. The quiet was uncanny. The only sound was an odd soft whine, like a kitten in pain.

Odette flashed her torch, and stared. There in the ice, caught as it was trying to fish, was a small otter. It must have been born in the late summer, thought Odette. She walked forward. As she had admitted, she did not normally care for animals, and avoided them whenever possible, but as she bent forward she found herself feeling intensely sorry for the poor, trapped animal. The cub was only the size of a young cat, and stared up at her with terrified brown eyes.

The ice was thick and difficult to chip. Odette searched round hurriedly till she found a rough, sharp stone.

The ice defied her. She beat at it with quick, tense movements, her breath coming hard in her throat from the bitter cold.

Suddenly the ice gave with a crack and a crump that flung her forwards, terrified, both hands in icy water. The otter sank. She gave a cry, but, hands frozen, groped in the black water, dropping her torch.

The cub stared up with terrified brown eyes

She felt its stiff body and lifted it out, some of the ice still adhering to its coat.

She began to think she would never reach the friendly lighted haven of the caravan that looked so cosy and welcoming now that she was outside in the icy wind and the dark.

She fell up the steps, battering the door, her hands too cold to turn the key.

"You silly girl," her father said. "What on earth have you been doing? Your coat-sleeves are soaked."

He came to help her with her coat. "Your hands are bleeding," he said. "Here, let me dry you."

Odette found her voice. "Quick, quick, do something," she said, and thrust the soaked and dripping bundle into her father's hands.

The cub was stiff, its eyes closed. The tiny openings of the rounded ears were filled with ice, the webbed feet scaly with frozen crystals, the long tail ramrod-stiff.

"I don't know if we can save him," her father said. "We'll try. It's the best we can do."

Odette rubbed her hands dry on a towel. Feeling had gone from them and they were purple and bleeding.

The little otter lay on her father's lap, wrapped in a warm towel. Her father began to rub the stiff coat dry. He rubbed until the frozen water had melted and the coat was soft again, but the otter did not move.

"He must live, he must!" said Odette desperately. "I can keep him if he does, can't I?"

Odette's mother warmed some milk and then poured it into the little beast's mouth, but it did not swallow. Her father tried to force the liquid into its throat by stroking the throat muscles downwards, but there was not a sign of movement.

He held a mirror in front of the cub's mouth. A faint mist clouded it.

"He's still alive," he said.

He put the otter on the rug in front of the stove, and began to massage its body.

"Could you have him till I get back?"

"I'm afraid it's useless," her father said.

"We can't give up," Odette said. "Please go on, Daddy—please!"

There was a knock at the door.

Her father opened it, and found one of his men standing on the step, a big alsatian dog beside him.

"My wife had to go into hospital to have her baby," he said. "We don't know what to do with Kim. I hate to ask, but could you have him till I get back?"

"Yes, of course," said Odette's mother.

"Now, you be good," he added to the dog. He turned to Odette's father. "I'll be off, and thank you. His food's here."

He handed in a sack full of tins of dog meat.

Before any of them could do anything, the big dog walked over to the hearth and sniffed at the baby otter. Then it settled down on the hearthrug in front of the stove, the cub tucked tightly against its body. It began to lick the cub.

Odette watched, fascinated. The dog licked continuously, the warm tongue covering every inch of the tiny body until the fur was wet and standing on end. The cub whimpered.

The alsatian worked on. Ten minutes later its efforts were rewarded and the otter cub opened it eyes.

"Talk to it very gently," Odette's father said. "A soft voice means more than anything to a wild animal. Remember he's small and terrified."

She began to talk gently to the cub, and rubbed its fur dry. Her mother brought the warmed-up milk. They set the little animal down on the hearth and held the saucer in front of it. It turned its head away.

Kim came over and took a lick from the saucer. The cub watched suspiciously, and then lapped slowly, surprised. It finished the plateful, and whimpered.

"Try it with tinned fish," her mother suggested.

The cub could scarcely wait when it smelled the food and yickered excitedly until it was put down.

Odette found the days that followed passed too quickly. The otter learned to follow her around. Kim's owners moved their caravan so that Odette's mother was handy to help with the new baby, and Kim himself shared both homes, but preferred to play with the otter whenever he got the chance.

By Christmas Day Odette was hand-feeding stags, and had added a squirrel to her family.

"You know," said Odette, "I didn't think life could be such fun out in the wilds."

Her father laughed. "Baden-Powell knew it could be," he said. "That was one of the reasons why he founded the Guide and Scout Movement. I was a Scout, you know. You're just beginning to catch the spirit of Guiding, Odette, and you've got your otter to thank for it."

Odette nodded. "I'm glad I found him. He's taught me a lot—yes, even about Brownie Guiding."

The Smallest Bulbul

A True Brownie Story by PAT SHARPE

Far away in South India there was a Pack of Brownies, but they weren't called Brownies in India, but Bulbuls.

Chota was the smallest Bulbul in the Flock, and this worried her very much. Most of the other Bulbuls were very kind, but a few of them teased her and called her a dwarf.

Chota wasn't a dwarf; she simply hadn't grown at the usual rate. Her real name wasn't Chota; it was Rani (which means Queen), but she was nicknamed Chota, which means "small".

Because of her size Chota found it difficult to keep up when her Flock competed in sports and running games, and this made her unhappy because she felt she was letting down her Six.

"Don't worry, Chota," her Flock Leader (Brownie Guider) would say kindly. "It really doesn't matter a bit. Remember how good you are at other things!" Chota was indeed very quick at signalling and first-aid and knots. She had more badges than anyone else in her Six.

One day Flock Leader told the Flock that she had arranged to take them on an all-day picnic up in the mountains. They were to go by train and camp for a day on a coffee plantation. They were all very excited about this outing and talked of nothing else for days before. Then, two days before the trip, Chota overheard two of the Bulbuls talking, not realising she was within ear-shot.

The Bulbuls ate vegetable curry off banana leaves

"It's a pity we have to take Chota," said one of them. "She'll slow everything up so! Flock Leader is always waiting for her to catch up."

Poor Chota's face went red, and she felt the tears smarting in her eyes. Next day she went to Flock Leader. "Please, I don't think I can come to the picnic tomorrow," she said.

Flock Leader looked at her shrewdly. "Why not, Chota?"

"Well, I—I——" Chota had meant to make some excuse, but found herself bursting into tears.

Flock Leader was very kind and understanding. She didn't ask any questions, but she persuaded Chota quite firmly to come!

It was fun winding up the steep mountain track in the funny little train. When they reached the station at the top of the mountain, the Bulbuls tumbled out excitedly with their packs on their backs. They had to walk about a mile through the coffee plantation. Chota had never seen coffee growing before. It was blossom-time and on the dark-green bushes were sprays of sweet-smelling white flowers rather like jasmine, which later on would turn into bright-red berries.

"I thought it would smell like coffee," she said.

"Oh, no!" explained Flock Leader. "That smell comes only after the beans are dried and roasted."

There was a factory in the middle of the plantation where, about Christmas-time when the berries were ripe, they were brought in huge baskets to be "pulped" and washed and dried before being sent away to the shops to be roasted and ground. But now there was no work going on in this factory and the huge drying-grounds were empty. It was here that the Bulbuls were going to camp.

Everyone was soon busy picking up firewood and lighting fires. Presently a great earthenware pot of rice was bubbling away on one fire and a vegetable curry on the other. When it was ready, the Bulbuls sat around and ate it off banana leaves, which they cut into squares and which made lovely plates. They ate with the hands, as Indians do, using only the tips of their fingers so that the rest of their hands would not become greasy. After the curry and rice they had fresh fruit—delicious pineapples and oranges, which grew in their gardens. And then they lay in the warm sunshine, resting.

Suddenly this peaceful scene was shattered by a low rumble, and the ground began to tremble.

If you lived in India you would know what this meant—it was an earthquake, and it was frightening because there was nothing much anyone could do about it, except to stay out in the open so that nothing could fall on top of them.

Most of the girls had been in earthquakes before and no one screamed or panicked. They just watched the long "lines" of low buildings where the coolies lived rock and sway.

The coolies were all out on the plantation working. Only a few old women and children were left in the "lines", and they all came running out, shouting.

Presently one end of the building collapsed and an old coolie woman came screaming towards the Bulbuls.

"The baby!" she cried. "The baby! My grand-daughter—she's inside the house that has fallen in!"

The earthquake stopped as suddenly as it had begun.

Flock Leader and all the Bulbuls ran towards the "lines", where a crowd of children and a few old women were gathered round the collapsed house, shouting and crying.

From inside the house came a thin wail. The old woman explained that her daughter was out working and had left the baby in the house in the grandmother's charge.

"I was cooking," she sobbed. "The fire is alight in there. The baby will burn. There is no way to get her out! See, there is only that narrow entrance."

The roof had fallen in and a thin beam lay across the window, leaving only a very small opening through which wisps of smoke were coming. The door was entirely blocked by a pile of stones and mortar.

A small voice spoke. It was Chota's. "I can wriggle in, I think," she said.

Flock Leader looked doubtful. "The whole thing may collapse on

"There is no way to get her out!"

you, dear," she warned, "and you may suffocate with the smoke. I'm responsible for you, and I can't allow you to risk your life."

But for once Chota didn't obey Flock Leader. She was already scrambling up to the window and trying to wriggle through the narrow space. Squeezing and pushing, she at last succeeded, and half fell into the little room.

Groping her way through the smoke, coughing and spluttering, she made her way to where the baby's wails came from, and, feeling about in the darkness, found the child. She picked it up and groped her way again to the opening, pushing the baby through first.

Eager hands seized it, and then Chota, almost overcome by smoke, eased herself back through the opening—back into the fresh clean air again—spluttering and choking as she fell into Flock Leader's arms.

They crowded round her then, the old coolie woman and the children and the whole Bulbul Flock, thanking her and congratulating her on saving the baby's life.

Chota smiled through her coughs. "At last," she choked happily, "at last I'm glad I'm so small!"

Brownies in the Enchanted Wood

by TILLY WINGRAVE

"Only one more day left!" sighed Sue, staring out of the window.

"But we've had a lovely time," said Mandy, perched on the edge of her bed, "even if it has rained every day."

"We haven't had a chance to explore the enchanted wood," grumbled Sue, looking across the wide lawn of the Brownie Pack Holiday House to the wood beyond.

"How do you know it's enchanted?" asked Mandy.

"I know!" replied her friend. "You only have to look at it to see that."

Privately, Mandy thought that Sue had rather too much imagination! Supposing she was right, though? It would be exciting to find out!

"Well," she said aloud, "you may get your chance tomorrow. The forecast is for fine weather, so Titania says we can go for a ramble in the woods with the Fairies."

"Titania" was the Brownie Guider. The "Fairies" were four Ranger helpers, who the Brownies called Peasblossom, Cobweb, Moth and Mustardseed, after the Fairy Queen's attendants.

The tinkling of handbells ("fairy music", the Brownies called it) put an end to thoughts of exploring, and the girls ran down to supper.

The next day was warm and sunny.

"Put on your wellingtons," said Titania, as the Brownies prepared for their ramble. "It's sure to be wet in the woods."

"You mean our magic seven-league boots," corrected Sue.

"Of course!" smiled Titania. "How silly of me!"

The Brownies set off across the gardens and into the woods, with Peasblossom and Mustardseed leading the way, Cobweb nearly halfway along the line, and Moth bringing up the rear.

As they reached the woods, Sue caught Mandy's hand and began to drop back.

"What are you doing?" asked Mandy, as Sue stooped and pretended to look at something on the ground.

"Shh!" hissed Sue.

She watched as the Brownies disappeared round a bend in the path. Moth was listening to something a small Brownie was telling her, and hadn't noticed the two girls falling behind.

Pulling Mandy after her, Sue dived down a side turning.

"Come on!" she said. "You want to find out if the wood is enchanted, don't you?"

Mandy nodded. "Yes, but I don't think we ought——" she began, but Sue was already hurrying down the path.

Mandy ran after her. She found it hard to keep up with her longlegged friend. Then, rounding a bend, she saw that Sue was nowhere in sight.

Which way should she go? Quickly Mandy made up her mind, and hurried along the path to her right. After some time the trees began to thin out, and she caught a glimpse of a building in a clearing.

"Good!" she thought. "I'm back at the House."

But when she emerged from the trees she saw to her amazement that the building was a castle!

Was the wood magic, after all?

She crept forward and peeped in through a window. What she saw made her gasp in astonishment.

Old King Cole sat on his throne, wriggling to get comfortable.

"Bring me my pipe!" he called.

He settled his crown more firmly on his head.

As he did so, a worried footman appeared.

"I'm very sorry, Your Majesty," he said. "I'm afraid there has been an accident. The page who was bringing your pipe was tripped up by one of the royal cats, and your pipe was broken."

"Oh, well, I suppose it can't be helped," said Old King Cole, who was clearly disappointed. "Bring in my bowl."

The doors of the Throne Room were flung open, and a very grand footman, carrying a magnificent silver punchbowl, came slowly down the room.

Mandy gave a gasp of horror as the footman caught his toe in the edge of the beautiful scarlet-and-gold carpet, and fell flat on his face. The punch spilled out in all directions!

"Bother!" grumbled Old King Cole. "Ah, well, send in my fiddlers three!"

There was a long pause, and then came the sound of raised voices in the distance. At last, after quite a time, the footman came back. He looked very red and flustered.

"Well," said the King, "where are they?"

"Er—I'm afraid——" began the footman.

"Where are they?" King Cole demanded. He was getting quite upset.

"I'm afraid they're on strike, Your Majesty," answered the footman nervously.

"Oh, bother, BOTHER!" Now King Cole looked really cross. "This is really too bad!" He sat with his chin in his hand, not looking at all like the Merry Old Soul he was supposed to be.

Mandy felt very sorry for him. "I wish I could help," she thought.

Then an idea came to her. She began to creep round the castle, peeping through windows as she went. It wasn't long before she found the castle kitchen. Slipping in through an open door, she spoke quickly to the plump, rosy-cheeked woman inside.

Five minutes later she was back outside the Throne Room window.

"Now," she thought, "I hope the King is watching."

The punch spilled out in all directions!

Old King Cole looked up. Something bright and shining was floating past the window. Looking out, he saw Mandy, with a clay pipe and a bowl of soapsuds, blowing bubbles.

"My word, that looks fun!" cried the King. He stepped out into the garden to have a closer look. "I suppose you haven't got a spare pipe?" he asked Mandy wistfully.

"Why, yes, Your Majesty, I have!" replied Mandy, and she held up a second clay pipe, which the royal cook had given to her with the bowl of soapsuds.

Old King Cole sat down on the grass beside Mandy. Soon each was happily trying to blow bigger and finer bubbles than the other.

"You know," said King Cole, after a time, "this really is fun. All I miss now is the music of my fiddlers three."

Without a word, Mandy reached into her pocket, and brought out the little transistor radio that Mummy and Daddy had given her for her birthday. The cheerful sound of music filled the castle garden. Soon the Queen and her ladies, and all the courtiers, came out to listen.

Hearing the music, the fiddlers three came into the garden. They were soon playing happily, their strike forgotten.

Old King Cole blew an extra fine stream of bubbles. "You know," he said, watching the Queen and her ladies dancing, "this has turned out to be the merriest day I have ever spent!"

Picking up her radio, Mandy slipped away unnoticed into the wood.

When Sue realised that Mandy was no longer following, she at once turned back to look for her. In and out of the trees she hurried, but there was no sign of her friend. Not only that, before long she herself was completely lost!

At last she heard footsteps hurrying towards her. To her relief, round a bend in the path came Mandy.

"Oh, Sue," cried Mandy, as soon as she was near enough, "I've had such an adventure!"

Sue was both pleased and disappointed when she heard her friend's story.

A flock of blackbirds flew from an open window

"I knew the wood was enchanted!" she cried. "But I wish I had been with you," she added wistfully.

"It must be nearly lunch time," said Mandy. "Which is the way back?"

"I don't know," Sue confessed. "I'm lost. Let's try this way."

The two girls set off, but the path they were following seemed to twist and turn on itself, taking them deeper and deeper into the wood.

Suddenly Sue ran forward. "Look!" she cried. "We're back at your castle!"

"Wait!" called Mandy. "It's not the same one!"

As the Brownies stared at the castle's greystone walls—

"Oh, no—not again!" cried a voice, and a flock of blackbirds flew from an open window, and disappeared above the trees.

Moments later, a figure in velvet and ermine and wearing a gold crown ran from the door and stood watching the birds as they flew away.

"Can we help you, Your Majesty?" asked Sue politely.

"It really is too bad!" grumbled the King. "Just because I was pleased when the cook put four-and-twenty live blackbirds in the pie on my birthday she does it every week!" He straightened his crown. "After all," he went on, "when you're feeling hungry it's not very nice to see your dinner flying out of the window!"

"Come back to our Pack Holiday House and have lunch with us," said Sue impulsively. "I know Titania will be pleased to see you."

"Thank you—that's very kind of you!" replied the King. "Which way do we go?" He was obviously hungry!

"Oh dear, I forgot!" gasped Sue. "We're lost!"

"You need never be lost in the enchanted wood," answered the King. "Just stand one on each side of me, and hold my hands. Now think hard of the place you want to go to." The Brownies gripped the King's hands "Keep your eyes shut tight," he warned.

As the girls closed their eyes, they felt wind rushing past their faces; then there was a gentle bump.

"Now open your eyes," said the King.

The King insisted on sitting between his new friends!

To their surprise, the Brownies found themselves, still clutching the King's hands, walking along the path which led to the garden of the Pack Holiday House. Ahead they could see the rest of the Pack. Moth was still listening to the small Brownie.

Cobweb dropped back to speak to Moth. "Don't let the Brownies dawdle," she said. "We don't want to be late today. Lunch on the last day of a Pack holiday is always fun."

This was Moth's first Pack holiday. "Why," she asked, "what happens?"

"Miss Andrews, the District Commissioner, always comes," answered Cobweb. "She's great fun. She always dresses up as a fairy-tale character, and really enters into the spirit of things. Then, after lunch, she slips away before the Brownies find out who she really is." Cobweb looked round. "Where's that tall chatterbox and her little friend?" she asked anxiously.

"Here they come now," said Moth, as Sue and Mandy rounded the last bend. "But who's that with them?"

"It must be Miss Andrews," said Cobweb. "I suppose she came through the woods to meet us. She does look funny with whiskers."

Back at the house, the warm smell of lunch met them at the door. Mandy and Sue were most surprised to find that their guest seemed to be expected. Afterwards, the King drew them to one side.

"That was delicious," he said, "but I must hurry away now. I have a busy afternoon in the counting-house."

After the Pack had gone upstairs for the quiet hour, Moth gave a gasp.

"Oh, dear, I forgot!" she said to Titania. "A letter came for you by hand, just before we went out. I'll go and fetch it, shall I?"

She ran into the hall, and picked up an envelope from the brass tray on the table.

Titania opened it. "Why," she exclaimed, "it's from Miss Andrews! She says she won't be able to come to lunch today."

She looked up from the letter and stared at the Rangers.

"If she couldn't come," she said slowly, "*who was it the Brownies brought to lunch!*"

The New Brownie

by DOROTHY PEARCE

Modupe never carried her books and pencils to school in a case. She set off each morning with them perched on her head.

Modupe lived with her mother, Mrs. Adunle, and her two brothers, Fidelis and James, just outside Lagos, in Nigeria.

Each morning Mrs. Adunle went to market, with baby James sleeping comfortably on her back, the way Nigerian babies do. Fidelis, a sturdy boy of three, trotted at her side. In the market she sold bowls of peppery soup and balls of dumpling-like dough called fufu to eat with the soup.

Modupe helped her mother make the fufu each evening. It had to be pounded in a great wooden bowl with a long stick. Modupe and Mother sang a song as they pounded, almost dancing round the big bowl.

As the market was halfway to school, the whole family set off each morning together. As far as the market Modupe carried on her head the little stool on which Mother sat all day, as well as her school books. With baby James securely tied on her back, Mother balanced the big bowl of fufu balls on her head, while Fidelis proudly trotted behind with a pile of banana leaves on his head. In the market his job was to wrap each fufu ball in a banana leaf, ready for the customers. They were a merry party, laughing and

The whole family set off each morning together

talking and shouting to friends whom they met on the road.

After school Modupe went back to the market. Going home, she usually carried James on her back, for Mother often had to carry Fidelis, who was tired after a long day in the hot sun.

One day the school headmistress came to Modupe's class to tell them some good news.

"We have a new teacher who knows all about Brownie Guides. Tomorrow she will tell you what Brownie Guides are and about the Brownie Guide Pack she wants to run for you. She will be called Brown Owl, and you children will be the Brownie Guides. It is great fun and at the same time you will learn many useful things."

Modupe ran all the way to the market that afternoon to tell Mother the good news.

When Mother heard that Brownie Guides would be after school hours, she shook her head and told Modupe she would not be able to be a Brownie Guide as she had to help with the children when school finished.

Modupe was sad at this, but she knew Mother worked very hard to send her to school at all, so she tried not to show how disappointed she was.

Modupe was the only one in the class who was not a Brownie. Her friends teased her when she said she wasn't joining. Modupe pretended she wasn't interested in Brownies, so that they wouldn't think Mother was stopping her. All the same, the night of the first Brownie meeting she did wish she too was staying for it. She tried not to think about Brownies as she walked home with James asleep on her back.

Next day the others were full of tales of the lovely time they had had and all that Brown Owl had told them they would be doing. They laughed and called Modupe "a silly old stay-at-home".

Brown Owl heard them teasing Modupe. Next meeting she said she had an important thing to tell them, so they must hold a Pow-wow. She explained that what they were going to talk about was a Brownie secret and mustn't be discussed anywhere else afterwards.

"We have a new teacher who knows all about Brownie Guides"

"I know Modupe would love to be a Brownie, but she can't be because she has to help with her brothers in the market each afternoon. So, you see, she is already doing a good turn each day without the fun of being a Brownie. We mustn't tease her, but must try to help her share our Brownie fun. Perhaps one day she'll be able to be a Brownie too."

The Brownies thought hard about this. Then the two new Sixers had an idea. They asked if they might teach Modupe Brownie work and games during playtime.

Brown Owl thought that would be splendid. "It is a very good idea to teach her; then she will be ready to join one day."

So the Sixers taught Modupe lots of Brownie work and played the new games with her in the playground.

Children in Nigeria, where it is very hot, mostly sleep on mats on the floor instead of in beds. One of the first things Brown Owl taught the Brownies was that it was important to air their bedmats each morning, then to roll them up instead of just leaving them on the ground.

Mother thought this was a good thing when Modupe told her, so each morning Modupe hung the mats in the sun.

The Brownie Promise ceremony was fixed for the first meeting after the Easter holidays. Everyone was excited about it, but poor Modupe felt sadder than ever.

At the last meeting before the holidays the Sixers asked for a special Pow-wow.

"Please, Brown Owl, we've had another idea," one of them said. "If we went to the market in turn to help Mrs. Adunle, Modupe could come to the meeting and make her Promise with us."

Brown Owl was very pleased at this.

"I'll do something to help too," she said. "We'll have three extra meetings during the Easter holidays to make sure Modupe is ready to make her Promise."

"Will you tell her, Brown Owl?"

"I'd like you to, as it was your idea. Perhaps I'll come along with you too."

"After she's made her Promise, the whole Pack want to take turns with Modupe in helping Mrs. Adunle. That will only mean that each one will miss one meeting in fourteen, as there will be fourteen of us then."

"You have fixed everything well. I am proud of you," said Brown Owl, smiling.

Modupe was delighted when she heard the news. The Sixers went with her to tell her mother.

Mother was quite happy with the new plan.

"I did so want Modupe to be a Brownie, but I couldn't think of a way out. You're all very clever. It seems to me that Brown Owl has taught you a great deal in a short time. Thank you for finding a way for Modupe to join."

Brownie in Secret

by SHEILA HIBBERT

"There's going to be a Brownie Pack in the village, and I'm going to join!" Janet clapped her hands in glee and hopped first on one foot and then on the other. "Are you going to join, Brenda?"

Brenda scuffed the ground with the toe of her shoe as they walked home from school together. "I don't know. I'll have to ask Mummy."

"It's going to be such fun. There'll be meetings in the village hall every Tuesday from six o'clock until half past seven. Miss Jones is going to take us—only we shan't call her Miss Jones, but Brown Owl or another name like that!"

Brenda had heard all this in school. She liked Miss Jones, and Anna, Tracy, Sarah and Emma were all going; but when she had mentioned it her mother hadn't really seemed to be listening.

"The first meeting's tomorrow," Janet reminded Brenda. "You'd better tell your mum."

The two girls turned up a lane that ran through a little wood, then along a cart-track to a group of four pretty cottages that stood at the end. When Brenda ran in, her mother was laying the table for tea. She was hurrying, as usual, with quick looks at the clock on the mantelpiece. Brenda's tiny baby brother, Teddy, was sitting on the rug with some bricks, and her little sister, Eileen, was putting her dolly to bed.

"Mummy," said Brenda breathlessly, "you know I told you about the Brownies? Well, they're going to start tomorrow in the village hall. And Miss Jones has asked us again if we want to join. Can I, Mummy—oh, can I? Please say I can."

Mrs. Bell shook her head, taking a pie out of the oven. "No, Brenda; you're too young."

"But, Mummy, we can go if we are seven, and I'm seven-and-three-quarters!"

"Yes, but you've got to get back afterwards and I'm not having you walking through the wood alone in the dark. I can't leave the little ones to come and fetch you."

"But Janet is going, Mummy, and I could walk back with her."

"No, Brenda; it's no use. I would never know whether she would bring you or not. She's quite a bit older than you, and she might forget to wait for you. Now sit down and have your tea and we'll hear no more about it."

Mrs. Bell thought no more about the Brownies—she was always so busy, anyway—but Brenda did. When she saw Janet on the Wednesday after the meeting, she begged her to tell her all about it.

"What did you do?" she asked.

"Well, Miss Jones—I mean, Brown Owl—took our names and then we danced in the Brownie Ring and sang the Brownie song."

"Oh, teach me the Brownie song, Janet!"

So Janet sang:

"We're Brownie Guides, we're Brownie Guides,
We're here to lend a hand.
To love our God and serve our Queen
And help our homes and land.
We've Brownie friends, we've Brownie friends,
In North, South, East and West,
We're joined together in our wish
To try to do our best."

Then Brenda sang it with her, and learned the words.

"Then what did you do?" she asked.

"Well, Brown Owl told us a story about two children called

They went and found the owl

Tommy and Betty, who were lazy and wanted a Brownie to come and help in the house and do all the work to save them from having to do jobs. Then their mother told them to go into the wood and find the wise old owl, who would tell them where to find a Brownie. So they went and found the owl and she told them to look in a pool at moonlight and say:

'Twist me and turn me and show me the elf.

I looked in the water and there saw . . . . . .'

and see who they saw to make up the rhyme. So the girl went to look and all she saw was herself reflected in the pool. She went back to Mrs. Owl and told her and Mrs. Owl said: 'Would not the word "myself" make the rhyme?' She told her she could be a Brownie if she tried. She said that Betty and Tommy could get up early and bring in the wood and tidy the house and clean the shoes and lay the breakfast and all sorts of things—all in secret before anyone was up."

"Well," cried Brenda excitedly, "I could be a Brownie in secret, couldn't I?"

Janet looked a little bit doubtful.

"I could! I could!" insisted Brenda. "Mummy won't let me join properly, but I could be a secret Brownie! You can tell me all you learn and I'll try ever so hard! Oh, do let me, Janet—you must let me!"

At last Janet gave in. After that she and Brenda met whenever they could in the woodshed, and Janet would teach Brenda all that she had learned at the Brownie meeting.

First of all she taught her the Brownie Promise and the Law and the Motto. Then she taught her how to salute and shake hands the special Brownie way.

A few weeks later, Janet made her Promise. It was almost too much for Brenda to see her friend go off in her new Brownie uniform. When Janet came back she had a shiny silver Promise badge on her tie and a gay Imp Six emblem on her uniform. She was a real Brownie now.

Janet explained a lot of things to Brenda.

"Brown Owl says we mustn't just learn things to pass a Challenge and get a badge, but so that we can help at home. We promise to do a good turn every day."

"But what could I do?" asked Brenda.

"It doesn't have to be anything big. Just a small good turn that nobody has told you to do is best. You could wash up the tea-things, and put your toys away, or the baby's toys, and get wood in from the shed. At first we only do quite easy things, but later on we are going to do much harder things and I'll have to show you. That will be when we have got the Footpath badge and are working for the Road and the Highway badges."

Then Janet showed Brenda some of the games they had played and told her a story about Brownies in other countries all over the world, who sometimes had a different uniform and a different name but were Brownies all the same.

At home, Brenda didn't tell her mother about all this, but on Saturday morning she tidied up her bedroom and then turned out the little ones' playbox and tidied that.

Her mother said to her father at dinner: "Brenda's getting quite tidy at last."

Brenda said never a word!

After tea, her father had to go and shut up the hens and her mother went upstairs and put the little ones to bed, so Brenda carefully put the tea-things into the big bowl and filled it with hot water. When her mother came down, the tea-things were all washed, dried and put away.

Mrs. Bell was most surprised, but decided that Mr. Bell must have done it, for there was Brenda sitting by the fire, reading and saying not a word.

Janet was a very quick Brownie. Of course, she was older than most of the others, but it seemed no time at all before she had gained her Footpath badge and was working for the Road badge.

"It's fun being a Brownie," she told Brenda. "We've been cleaning shoes the proper way—look, I'll show you. You go and get a pair."

Brenda crept out of the woodshed and back to the house, where she found her mother's best brown shoes and her father's stout black ones. Janet brought some shoe-polish and brushes and a duster, and they set to work. After dinner on Sunday, her father said he was going for a walk and would like her mother to go with him—but he was in a hurry, as he wanted to see someone.

"I can't be ready very quickly," said Mummy. "My shoes are so muddy I'm afraid they will take ages to clean."

"I'll do them," said Daddy, but when he found them they were shining as brightly as polished chestnuts! So he put them ready, thinking Mummy had done them and forgotten all about it.

Still Brenda never told! Quietly and secretly she did all kinds of little jobs about the house—and Mummy began to look less tired.

Janet showed Brenda everything she had learned, and Brenda was sure that if she couldn't be a real Brownie this was the next best thing. After all, it was what Betty and Tommy in the story had done.

One day, little Eileen had had her hair washed and was drying it by the fire. Teddy, who was a very little boy, was playing with some soldiers on the mat. Then he tried to poke one through the wire mesh of the fireguard, saying that his hair wanted drying, too! But—oh, dear!—when he tried to pull the soldier back it caught in the wire, and the fireguard came unfastened and fell over. Then, before Brenda could cross the room to put it back, little Eileen leaned forward to pick it up and her nightie caught fire!

The burning flame sizzled the hem of the nightie. Eileen screamed and Teddy burst into tears. Brenda didn't stop to think or feel frightened. She rushed across the room, caught hold of Eileen, and rolled her in the mat, smothering the flames. Just as she was doing this, her mother rushed in. She ran over to Eileen, but Brenda had put out the flames and the danger was over.

Eileen was crying, but Brenda had put the flames out so quickly that she had only one tiny burn on her leg. Mummy had gone white, but she was very thankful as she put the little ones to bed.

When she came downstairs again, she said to Brenda: "You were a very sensible girl, Brenda, and brave, too. If you hadn't acted

Brenda rolled her in the mat, smothering the flames

quickly, Eileen might have—might have—" but she couldn't say it.

When Daddy came in, Mummy told him all that had happened. She was still pale.

"How did you know what to do so quickly?" Daddy asked, kissing Brenda.

Brenda couldn't keep the secret any longer! She told them about the Brownies and what Janet had taught her.

Suddenly Mrs. Bell's puzzled face broke out into a smile. "So it's you who has done all these odd jobs lately—brought in the wood and laid the table and cleaned my shoes?"

Brenda smiled and nodded.

"Well," said Mrs. Bell, "you have certainly opened my eyes about the Brownies—and you saved Eileen just now, all because you knew just what to do."

"It seems to me Brenda has been much wider awake than we have," remarked Mr. Bell, and Mrs. Bell nodded in agreement. "Well, what's our next move, do you think?" smiled Mr. Bell.

"I think we had better go down and see the Guider tomorrow and ask if she can find a place for you in her Brownie Guide Pack, Brenda," said Mrs. Bell.

"Oh, yes!" cried Brenda. "I know she's got a place for me. It'll be with Janet in the Imp Six!"

And Brenda was right. She became an Imp in Janet's Six.

Dilys and the Duckling

by JEAN HOWARD

Dilys was taking a short cut along the river-bank on her way home from school. She was hurrying because it was Brownies tonight, and she wanted to finish her homework before changing into uniform.

The Brownies were having a special meeting tonight, because it was the Pack's twentieth birthday, and they had invited the local Cub Scout Pack to join in their celebrations.

There was a cold east wind blowing, and the towpath was deserted except for a large family of ducks who crossed the road, slithered down the steep bank and plopped into the dark grey water.

Dilys was just about to walk on, after watching the stately procession, when she noticed one little fellow trying to catch up with the rest of the family. He seemed to have difficulty in walking across the sandy path. When she looked more closely she saw to her horror that he had become entangled in a length of fishing line! He must have snapped at a fisherman's fly. His head was being pulled sideways by a piece of line which had caught round his beak and then twisted over his back and round one leg. He looked in a very sorry state.

Dilys tried to catch him, but he took fright and hurtled in ungainly fashion down the steep bank and into the water, where, in

He hurtled down the steep bank and into the water

a lopsided way, he endeavoured to swim after the others, his head permanently turned towards the bank.

Suddenly Dilys remembered a quaint little prayer she had once read in a book, and she quoted it softly to herself.

"Dear God, protect all folk
who quack and everyone who
knows how to swim—Amen."

Although she knew that unless she hurried on she would be late for Brownies, Dilys couldn't ignore the duckling's plight. Perhaps she could be God's means of protecting this little quacking creature! She hurried back to a telephone kiosk and dialled the number of the local R.S.P.C.A. She had a twopenny piece in her pocket.

On making the connection, she put her twopence in the slot and described what she had seen on the river-bank. The R.S.P.C.A. inspector asked if she would wait on the bank until he arrived so that she could show him where to find the unfortunate duckling, so she ran back down the towpath and was just in time see the family of ducks disappear under a willow-tree.

She had a cold, lonely vigil, but after about ten minutes a Land-Rover approached with an R.S.P.C.A. inspector and another man in it. Dilys ran up to the Land-Rover and made herself known to the R.S.P.C.A. inspector. The inspector told her they had brought a rubber dinghy. This they launched from a small sandy bay, and paddled down to the willow-tree.

As they moved in towards the bank, parting the branches carefully, the ducks swam swiftly out into the stream and away, but the handicapped duckling was unable to follow and went round and round in circles. After several unsuccessful attempts, the R.S.P.C.A. men finally caught him and gently disentangled him from the line.

Dilys watched from the bank. To her delight, the duckling seemed to be unharmed, for as soon as he was put back in the water he swam happily off.

Although Dilys was taken home in the Land-Rover, she arrived nearly an hour late at Brownies. Fortunately a rather late start had been made, so there was still time for her to join in the fun.

She told Miss Baily, the Brown Owl, why she was late.

"I wish more people would help birds and animals when they see them in distress," said Miss Baily. "Well done, Dilys! We'll look on your own action as a very nice twentieth birthday present for the Pack!"

Jane Gets There on Time

by KATHLEEN M. DUNCAN

"Oh, dear!" said Brown Owl. "The Pixie Six looks like being the 'Pixie Four' now that Angela has left the Pack and Marjorie is going up to Guides. It's a pity, because we want to be smart for the District Competitions. You will try and be more punctual, won't you, Jane, or else half the time we shall have only the 'Pixie Three'!"

Jane hung her head. This was the third time running that she had missed the bus and not been in time for the Brownie Ring. It had been a lot easier when her friend Angela had come to Brownies too, and had called for her, but now Angela's parents had moved out of the district.

Worse than that, with Marjorie going, the Pixies would be without a Sixer, and Brown Owl had not said anything yet about choosing another one.

"I'll try awfully hard," decided Jane. "I'll polish my shoes the night before and iron my tie before I go to school. I really will be on time next week."

She ran off to practise ball-throwing with Tawny, glad to be doing something she could do really well. She had a splendidly straight aim, and sent the ball nine times out of ten through the small hoop that the Gnome Sixer held up.

"Well done!" said Tawny Owl. "I shall put you down for the ball-throwing demonstration, Jane. The Elves are doing semaphore, the Sprites are laying a table, and the Gnomes are going to use the big compass—so practise during the week, all of you." Then she added: "Don't be late on Saturday!"

Jane kept her word, and on Friday evening she polished her shoes and belt till they shone. Her Promise badge was rubbed over, her beret brushed, and her uniform ironed.

"You're going to stand waiting a long time for the bus," Mummy said as Jane came running downstairs on Saturday afternoon. "Won't you wait indoors another ten minutes? Even then you'll be early!"

But Jane wouldn't wait, and she ran down the road towards the bus stop. On the way she saw something that made her stop. On the branch of an apple-tree in a garden was a beautiful blue budgerigar.

"My goodness! I must go and tell the people!" thought Jane.

She ran to the front gate, and then to her dismay saw that the bungalow was empty. By this time some passers-by had noticed the budgie too.

"It ought to be caught, or it will die of cold tonight," said one.

"I'd have a try, only I haven't got time—" said another, and Jane thought, "I haven't got time, either. I might miss my bus if—"

Then she remembered that a Brownie lends a hand, and she also remembered that Mr. Hindly, who lived just round the corner, kept budgerigars. He would probably come and catch it.

Just then two little girls crossed the road to see what Jane was looking at.

"Could you stay here and watch this budgie for me?" Jane asked them. "I'm going to tell someone about it and it may fly off somewhere else while I'm gone."

The little girls nodded. Jane ran off and banged on Mr. Hindly's front door. The door was opened by old grandma Hindly. Jane explained about the budgie. "I thought it might be yours," she said, "but even if it isn't could Mr. Hindly catch it, please? I must go now or I shall miss my bus."

"My son's out," said old Mrs. Hindly, who didn't hear very well.

Mrs. Hindly hands Joey to Jane

"He hasn't lost any budgie; they're all here. Suppose you take our Joey in his cage and hold it near the tree. Maybe the stray will come down to talk to Joey and you will catch him."

"I've got to go to Brownies—" began Jane desperately, but the old lady didn't hear her, and went off to fetch Joey.

She handed the cage to Jane, and Joey, who was bright-green, stood on his head.

"Oh, dear, I can't bear to think of a little bird like this dying of cold, so I suppose I must try to catch it," thought Jane, wondering what she should do with the stray budgie if she did succeed in catching it, and what Brown Owl would say if she was late on this special day.

She hastened round the corner. To her surprise, she saw that one of the little girls had an empty cage in her hand.

"We've just moved into the house opposite," she explained to Jane. "This cage used to belong to our canary. Mummy thinks we might get the budgie to come into it. She's put some food on the floor."

Then Jane had an idea. "Let's tie the cages together," she said. "We can tie the door of this one open; then perhaps it'll walk in to see Joey. I'll tie them with my hankie. Can you lend me one of yours?"

"Here's mine too," said the other little girl. "I think the budgie is tired. Perhaps it's flown a long way. It hasn't moved since you went. It's pretty, and it's got a red ring on one leg."

Jane forgot all about Brownies as the three of them went into the garden of the empty bungalow and very slowly and quietly approached the tree.

"I'll climb up on to that low branch," whispered Jane. "You hand me up the cages." Carefully she climbed up, and then took the cages from the little girls.

Suddenly Joey began to say "Kissme . . . kissme! Pretty Joey!" loudly.

Jane held her breath. The blue budgie began to sidle down the branches.

At last he was on top of the cages. Jane was stiff and cramped, but she did not dare move. Then, to her joy, the little bird slid down the wire and ducked into the doorway. In a moment she put her hand over the opening.

"Got you!" she cried gleefully, and at that moment the red bus she was supposed to catch rumbled by. "Oh, dear, I shall be late again!" she cried.

The two little girls helped her down. As they were closing the cage door, they cried, "Here's Mummy!"

"I want to ask you about your Brownie Pack," their mummy said to Jane.

"Why," cried Jane, "are they Brownies too?"

"The twins were going to be," answered their mother, "but their daddy changed his job, and we moved here. I noticed you were in Brownie uniform, so I wondered whether they could go with you to Pack meeting and if there would be room for them in your Pack? They are just seven."

"Could they come now?" asked Jane eagerly. "It's a special day, and Mrs. Young, the District Commissioner, is going to be there. We'll have to walk all the way, though," she added, "because the bus has just gone, and I must take Joey back to Mrs. Hindly first. She lives at Number Three, round the corner."

"I'll take Joey back for you, and explain," offered the twins' mother. "I'd better take the stray budgie too. Perhaps Mrs. Hindly will know who owns it." Then she added: "You won't have to walk to wherever you're going. Here comes a relief bus. They're putting on extra ones today, because the circus is in town."

Jane was relieved and delighted. She would be in time, after all!

When she arrived at the Brownie hut, the twins, Sally and Anne, were with her, and they found the hut already full.

"Well done, Jane! You're just in time!" exclaimed Brown Owl. "We shall be starting a few minutes late because Mrs. Young has been delayed. Her budgie escaped half an hour ago, and she's trying to find out in which direction it flew—why, Jane, what is it?"

Excitedly, Jane told Brown Owl about her rescue of the budgie, and then she introduced the twins to her.

"Well, this is certainly your day!" exclaimed Brown Owl. "Mrs. Young's budgerigar is a show bird. She will be delighted when she hears it is safe. I'm glad too, and I'm very pleased that we have two new Brownies in the Pack."

"May they come in the Pixie Six, so that we aren't the 'Pixie Four' any more?" asked Jane eagerly.

"Of course they may," agreed Brown Owl, "and if you can be at Pack meetings on time in future I want you to be the Pixie Sixer!"

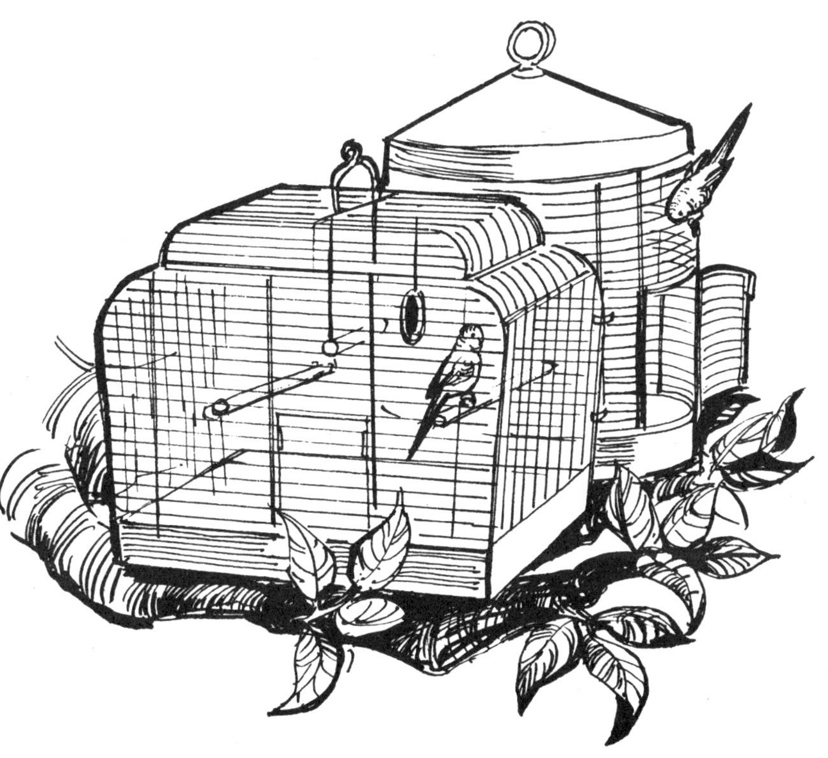

Television Capture

by ROBERT MOSS

"I'll be at the bus stop to meet you from Guides, Wendy," said Wendy Walker's father, who was kneeling behind the television set, doing something to the works.

"I hope you'll have fixed the TV set by then, Daddy. There's a programme I specially want to see."

"It'll be supper and bed for you as soon as you get in, you young scamp," retorted her father. "The chances are, anyhow, that the TV won't be behaving itself any better then than now. We haven't been free from interference a single night since we bought the set. I suppose it's all the cars we're getting through the village these days."

"There aren't many cars at night," said Wendy. "Perhaps washing machines and vacuum cleaners and spin-dryers and things like that cause the trouble."

"There aren't many housewives using washing machines and spin-dryers at night, either," grunted her father. "Well, you'd better pop off now, Wendy, or you'll be late for your precious Guide meeting."

Wendy had gone up to Guides only a fortnight before, and hadn't yet made her Promise. She had been in the Elf Six of her Brownie Pack, but now she was a proud member of the Kingfisher Patrol of a

Guide Company. The Kingfishers were the smartest Patrol in the Company, and for three years had held the shield awarded to the Patrol with top points. Wendy was very proud to belong to it, but was privately rather doubtful whether she'd ever manage to be a credit to it, as she wasn't gifted like Jenny Jordan, the Patrol Leader, or Margaret Pethwick, the Second.

Bidding her father goodbye, she stepped out into the dark country lane in which their cottage stood and hurried into the village, where the bus for Millhall was waiting.

"I ain't sure the bus'll be running tonight, missy," the bus conductor told her gloomily, as she climbed in. "Some of our chaps are on strike, an' we may get word any minute not to take the bus out."

"Oh, but I've got to get to Guides," cried Wendy in dismay, "and it's too far to walk!"

"Well, it ain't 'appened yet," the conductor told her kindly, "and if we don't 'ear something in the next few minutes we'll be off. Meself, I don't want to strike, but I got to if the rest does—see?"

Wendy nodded. She had only one concern—that was to get to the Guide Hut in Millhall in time for the meeting—and she breathed a sigh of relief when the bus-driver climbed into his seat and started up the engine. She fished in the pocket of her Brownie uniform for her fare.

"Well, we'll get you there, missy, but it's a toss-up whether there'll be a bus to bring you back from Millhall tonight," said the conductor, as he punched Wendy's ticket.

"Get me there—that's the main thing," said Wendy cheerfully.

Jenny greeted her with a smile when she stepped into the Guide Hut.

"Glad you were able to get here, Wendy. There was some talk of a bus strike, and I thought you might be cut off. Our Guider hasn't come yet, but she's got a car, so it can't be the strike. Have you ever played Kim's Game? No? Well, we'll see how good you are at it. It's a memory game, you know. It's fun."

Wendy proved to be quite marvellous at Kim's Game. She

"We'd better ask the way to Luscombe there"

remembered fifteen out of fifteen objects, then twenty-three out of twenty-five. The Assistant Guider, who took the meeting in the absence of the Guider, declared that Wendy was quite outstanding. Jenny was astounded.

Jenny's route home lay part of the way with Wendy's, and the two girls waited together at the bus-stop, talking—until at last Jenny realised she had been waiting very much longer than usual.

"I say, do you think the bus strike is on?" she asked Wendy. "The bus ought to have been here by now."

They waited a further fifteen minutes, then Jenny grimaced. "I'm afraid it's a long walk home for us, Wendy."

"We'd better start, then," said Wendy, rather anxiously. "Dad and Mum will worry if I'm not in to time."

"I'm afraid neither of us will be."

They set off briskly. When they reached the next hamlet, Begley, Jenny had an idea.

"There's a short cut over the fields to Luscombe, Wendy, and it'll be much quicker for you to get to Selcombe than going all the way by road." Jenny lived at Luscombe, which was about a mile from Wendy's home at Selcombe.

"If you're sure you know the way, it suits me," responded Wendy.

"Over the stile, then."

The night was moonless, and presently Jenny became unsure of her direction.

"I'm not sure I haven't gone wrong."

Wendy pointed. "Lights!" she exclaimed. "They must be the lights of Luscombe."

The lights were only pinpoints winking through a curtain of trees, but the Guides hurried towards them eagerly.

"Oh, it's only a building among the trees!" said Wendy disappointedly, halting suddenly.

She was right. The lights they had thought were those of Luscombe came from a farm outbuilding or group of sheds set back some distance from the track they were following.

"We'd better ask the way to Luscombe there," said Jenny.

Wendy nodded, then stopped and held up her hand. "Listen! What's that funny noise?"

A low droning sound, almost like the murmur of an aeroplane engine, buzzed through the silence of the night.

"It may be a generator making electricity for the farmhouse," said Jenny. "Come on—let's go and see."

When they reached the building, however, which was a big barn or timber shed, they had trouble finding an entrance in the dark. Through a chink in the wall, Wendy peered in.

"It's a garage, by the look of it. There are cars in it being repaired."

Jenny squinted through the chink. "It's that electric spraying machine they're using that's making the droning noise. We'd better find the door and ask our way."

They were still searching for the door when suddenly a harsh voice behind them made them both jump.

"What are you doing here? What d'you want?"

Both girls swung round. Through the gloom they could make out the figure of a powerfully built man.

"Gosh!" exclaimed Wendy. "You did make me jump!"

"We were trying to find a door to ask the way to Luscombe," Jenny told him.

"If you're going to Luscombe what are you doing here? You're well off the road and you're trespassing. You're nearer Selcombe. Luscombe's right the other side of the woods."

"We lost our way tramping across the fields," explained Wendy.

"There wasn't a bus back from Millhall because of a strike," added Jenny.

"I see." The voice was less harsh and suspicious now. "Well, you're very near Selcombe. I'll show you the track to it."

Gladly the Guides followed the big man, who led them alongside one wall of the shed and showed them a track running along the edge of a wood. As they passed through a pool of light that filtered on to the ground from a high window they saw the big man clearly for a moment. He was wearing a boiler-suit and had a tangled mop

"Gosh! You did make me jump!"

of ginger hair on a bullet-shaped head.

"Luscombe is on the far side of this wood," he told them. "Off you go, and mind you don't come this way again—it's private land."

The two girls set off thankfully along the path, watched by the big man.

They reached Selcombe in quite a short time. There, Wendy invited Jenny into her house. Her elder brother, who was a Venture Scout, offered to see Jenny home after she had sat down for refreshment.

"I say, Daddy," said Wendy, after she had told the family of the evening's adventure, "do you think that electric spraying machine, or whatever it was Jenny saw, could be the thing that causes the trouble with our TV?"

"By George, that's an idea!" agreed her father. "You say the place isn't far away, Wendy? If the machine is a powerful one I dare say it could affect sets in the village here. I must ask somebody about it who understands the working of television."

By the time the next Guide meeting came round the bus strike was over. The Guider was at the Guide Hut this time when Wendy got there.

"I couldn't get here last week," she explained to the Company. "When I went to get my car it had gone—yes, stolen! I haven't seen it since. I had to come by bus tonight. I hope to goodness the police trace it, but the chances are pretty thin now that I shall ever see it again. There's been quite a wave of car thefts all over the county. I'd be obliged if you'd all keep an eye open for it as you go about, Guides, and tell a policeman at once if you spot it."

"What is the number?" asked Linda Markham, Second of the Owls.

"The number's 1099 KFG," the Guider told her, "but it isn't likely to keep it. The first thing car thieves do is to change the number plate. They—why, is something up, Wendy?"

Wendy had put her hand up and was looking excited.

"Please," she said, "did you say 1099 KFG?"

"I did," answered the Guider, puzzled. "Why, Wendy? Have you seen it on the road since last week?"

"Yes—I mean, no—I mean, not on the road. I saw that number in the shed we looked in when we lost our way across the fields from Begley last Tuesday."

"What do you mean—you saw the number?" inquired Jenny, puzzled, turning to Wendy.

"I saw that number—1099 KFG—on a number-plate that was standing against a wall in the shed. I remember it because I thought how funny it would have sounded if it had been 1066—you know, the Battle of Hastings."

The Guider walked over to Wendy. She was looking serious. Wendy, who was the only girl in Brownie uniform, was feeling rather the odd girl out among the mass of Guide blue and was grateful when Jenny spoke up.

"Wendy and I took a wrong turning crossing the fields to Luscombe. We peeped into a big shed, because we wanted to ask our way."

"And that's where I noticed the number-plate," added Wendy.

"But what about the number?" asked the Guider. "Can you be quite sure it was 1099, with KFG after it?"

Wendy nodded vigorously. "Yes, I'm quite sure," she asserted.

"Wendy played Kim's Game last week," put in the Assistant Guider, "and she startled us with her amazing memory. I don't think she's likely to have made a mistake over a number-plate when she got twenty-three objects right out of a possible twenty-five at her first try."

"This is very interesting," said the Guider. "Carry on with the meeting, will you, Tessa? I'm going out to find a phone. The police may think this worth looking into."

The police thought it was well worth looking into. At the end of the meeting Wendy and Jenny had the thrill of stepping from the Guide Hut into a police-car in which sat a sergeant and three constables. The Guider squeezed in with them.

"Now young lady," said the police-sergeant to Wendy, "tell us exactly where this shed of yours was."

At their heels raced Wendy

"We can lead you to it, can't we, Jenny?" said Wendy.

Jenny nodded. "The quickest way will be from Selcombe," she said.

Never had two Guides experienced a more exciting night adventure than Wendy and Jenny. They padded, soft-footed, alongside the dark wood from Selcombe, with the policemen and their Guider in single file behind them. Tiny patches of light flickered into view through the trees as they approached the shed.

"There it is!" whispered Wendy, as the dark bulk of the building loomed up ahead.

"You and Green slip round the other side, Cox," ordered the sergeant. "Johnson and I will take the front door. Mind you don't charge them with wrongdoing until we're sure we haven't come on a wild-goose chase. Heh, where's that girl gone?"

In her eagerness, Wendy had not stopped when the police had. She had gone silently on to the shed. Now she was peering through the crack in the side of the shed through which she had looked before.

Now, however, she couldn't stop herself. She let out a loud yell.

"Quick! Help!" she shouted. "My daddy's in there—tied up!"

After that, things moved with violent speed.

"Come on!" called the police sergeant. "No need to wait now. Rush the door!"

Wendy was already at the door, beating on it with her fists and shouting: "We're coming, Daddy! The police are here!"

Whether the men inside heard the words or merely the hammering on the door, they took instant fright.

"Douse those lights!" snarled a voice.

The lights blinked out—but not all of them. There were several inspection-lamps in the place, and before these could be switched off the police were in. Headed by the sergeant, they burst the main door open. At their heels raced Wendy, who overlooked the dangers in her anxiety to reach her father, who was bound hand and foot and was about to be hoisted into the back of a blue saloon car.

The five men in the shed, the leader of whom was the big man who had come up behind the Guides the previous week, fought desperately, but the police soon had them helpless in handcuffs.

"My goodness, am I pleased to see you, Wendy!" gasped her father, as Wendy and Jenny cut at the ropes that bound him. "How you two girls come to be here I don't know, but you've brought the police in the nick of time. Those scoundrels were going to take me away in a car. They're car-thieves, and I'd seen too much for their liking."

"But whatever were you doing here, Daddy?" cried Wendy.

"What do you think? I came to see if I could stop the interference on our TV, of course! Don't you remember you said yourself that the electric spraying machine Jenny had seen in the shed might be the cause of all the trouble we've had with the TV, so tonight I thought I'd come and investigate. A car drove into the place just as I got here, and so I followed it in—and didn't come out again."

"And the car was a stolen one," said the police-sergeant, coming up. "Now, thanks to your clever Brownie daughter——"

"I'm a Guide now," put in Wendy swiftly.

"I beg your pardon—clever Guide daughter——" the sergeant corrected himself, smiling, "who remembered the number on a car-plate she saw here, we've run a whole dangerous gang of car-thieves to earth. They brought stolen cars here, changed their number-plates, and disguised them with new paintwork. Last week, unluckily for them, they brought in the Girl Guide leader's car, and at the Guide meeting tonight Wendy here heard the registration number and identified it as the very one she'd seen lying on the floor of this shed last week. What d'you think of that?"

"I think it's magnificent—that's what I think," said Wendy's father. "I'll make sure Wendy gets to Guides every week after this, bus strike or not!"

"Don't forget how Jenny helped, will you, Daddy?" put in Wendy, shyly.

"Indeed I shan't," said her daddy.

"I shan't forget, either," said the Guider. "You've been the means of getting my car back, for which I'm very grateful indeed."

"My goodness, am I pleased to see you, Wendy!"

"It was Wendy's show, really," Jenny said generously. "It was being an expert at Kim's Game that did the trick." She turned to Wendy. "Margaret Pethwick said she's jolly glad you've come into the Kingfishers, Wendy. So am I!"

"So am I," said Wendy happily.

A Pet for Pauline

by FREDA M. HURT

The two Brownies almost pressed their noses against the glass of the pet-shop window in their eagerness to see. They always stopped on the way to and from the Pack meeting to look in the pet-shop.

"Aren't they the darlingest things you ever saw?" cried Janice Janes, with a sigh of rapture.

"Yes," agreed Pauline Huggins. "I like the ginger one best."

"Yes, so do I." Janice jostled Pauline a little, in order to get closer to the cage in which the three kittens played. She waggled a finger against the glass, and the ginger-coloured one pretended it was a butterfly, and patted its side of the window with tiny paws.

"Oh, I wish he was mine! Don't you wish he was yours?" cried Janice.

"Rather," mumbled Pauline, who couldn't say all she felt.

"The two tabbies are perfectly sweet too, but the ginger one——" Even Janice, the chatterbox, could not find words to show how she felt about the ginger kitten.

It was sleek rather than fluffy, with a wee white chin and a white patch on its tummy. Its eyes were still a milky blue, and, in spite of being shut up in a cage, it seemed to be finding life an amusing game. While the Brownies watched, it chased its wisp of a tail, wrestled with its tabby brothers, pounced on imaginary mice, then

"Tabby with the white paws," she said

nosed the glass in front of Pauline and Janice in the friendliest manner.

"Oh, you little love!" exclaimed Janice, and though Pauline only smiled she was staring at the kitten with longing eyes.

Janice, who was Sixer of the Gnomes, was one of a family of three children, and she had an old dog, a white rabbit, and a tame tortoise at home. The dog belonged to the whole family, and the rabbit belonged to her brother Tim, but the tortoise was her very own. In her heart, Pauline envied her. She was an only child, and lived alone with her mother in a small flat. She had no pet at all, not even a white mouse. Her mother said they couldn't keep pets in a small flat with no garden of their own. But how Pauline wished she could have the ginger kitten!

"I could go in for the Animal Lover badge if I had it," she said. "I can't gain the Animal Lover badge without a pet to look after."

A stout, kind-looking woman joined them outside the shop. "The little dears!" she murmured, beaming at the kittens. Then she went into the shop.

"I believe she's going to buy one," whispered Janice, excitedly. "If it's the ginger one I shall ask her if I can stroke it."

Pauline said nothing, but she almost held her breath as the stout woman came to the door with the white-coated shopman and pointed to the kittens.

"Only twenty-five pence, eh?" she said. "Let me see, which one shall I have?"

"Not the ginger kitten, please, not the ginger kitten!" Pauline was saying to her in her own mind. She wanted it for herself so badly. Perhaps if she were to tell her mother just how much she wanted it she would say she could have it.

The stout woman made up her mind suddenly. "Tabby with the white paws," she said. "They say tabbies make good mousers."

Pauline let her breath out again in a sigh of relief. After they had seen the chosen kitten taken from the cage, and had stroked it in the woman's arms outside the shop, the Brownies tore themselves away and went home.

Pauline found her Aunt Muriel at the flat. She was a fussy person, but kind.

"Dear me, it's Christmas the week after next," she said, after she had remarked that "somebody's" shoes made a lot of noise, and "somebody's" hands needed washing. "How it does come round!"

Pauline was looking forward to Christmas, although she knew she would get nothing very exciting in the way of presents. Some of her friends had gifts like bicycles and expensive dolls, but Pauline's mother was a widow, and couldn't afford such things.

"And what would you like me to give you?" asked Aunt Muriel. "Something not *too* expensive," she added hastily.

"Please, I'd like a kitten," Pauline blurted out. "There's a ginger one in the pet-shop along the High Street, and it's only twenty-five pence." She looked eagerly from Aunt Muriel to her mother.

"Now, Pauline!" Mrs. Huggins sounded annoyed. "I've told you again and again that we cannot have a pet while we're living in this tiny flat."

"But, Mummy——" Pauline began to plead.

"No, Pauline." Mrs. Huggins, who was feeling cross and tired after a hard day's work, cut her short. "I don't want to hear anything more about it."

Pauline gulped and was silent. "It's not fair," she told herself, thinking of Janice's home and all the pets there. "It simply isn't fair."

She was grateful to Aunt Muriel, however, when she pressed some coins into her hand before she left. "That's for somebody's Christmas expenses," Aunt Muriel murmured, "in advance—and don't," she added, turning to Mrs. Huggins, "don't make her put it in her money-box."

"All right," smiled Pauline's mother, "though I expect she'll spend it on something quite silly. Children always do."

What should she spend it on? A book? Doll's furniture? A new pen? She had twenty-five pence from Aunt Muriel. The next day she was peering into shop windows with Janice, but she couldn't make up her mind.

"Let's go and see if those kittens are still in the pet-shop," suggested Janice, as they came away from Pack meeting the following Friday.

"All right," agreed Pauline, feeling the twenty-five pence in the purse on her uniform belt.

They went round to the pet-shop, and there were the two kittens curled into furry balls, asleep. The ginger one woke up when it heard the Brownies' voices, and looked at them with its head on one side, as if to say, "Hullo! So it's you two again!"

"What a shame your mother won't let you have him!" cried Janice. "After all, you could buy him with your money. You've got twenty-five pence."

Yes, she had enough. Pauline looked longingly at the ginger kitten, who started playing with a straw.

"I say!" cried Janice suddenly, excitedly. "Couldn't you buy him and keep him at *our* place?"

"At your place?" Pauline stared at her blankly.

"Yes. You could come and see him every day there, and perhaps your mother will soon change her mind about letting you have a pet, and then you can take him home."

"But what would *your* mother say?" Pauline frowned, secretly very tempted.

"Well——" Janice hesitated. "She needn't know about it," she said at last. "We could keep him in the shed at the bottom of the garden, where Arthur's hutch is." Arthur was the white rabbit.

"It wouldn't work," said Pauline. "She'd find out."

"She wouldn't," said Janice eagerly. "She hardly ever goes down the garden—not right to the end. And, anyway, she doesn't notice things very much. She's always so busy. I say, Pauline, you could work for your Animal Lover badge then."

Pauline still hesitated. And then a rather unpleasant-looking man stopped and stared in at the kittens. Pauline suddenly thought: "Suppose he buys the ginger kitten and isn't kind to it?" The idea was unbearable. "Come on!" she said to Janice, and ran into the shop. She offered her money and asked for the ginger kitten before she had time to think again and change her mind.

The shopman put the furry mite into Pauline's eager hands with instructions to take it straight home. Pauline came out of the shop in a kind of dream. Janice was pleased and admiring, and a little fearful now that the deed was actually done. Pauline buttoned the kitten inside her uniform. It pricked her skin as it clung to her vest with sharp little claws and mewed faintly. She stroked its tiny head with two fingers, and felt a thrill to think that she had a pet of her very own at last.

"I shall call him Rusty," she told Janice.

They smuggled Rusty into the shed at the bottom of Janice's garden, without being seen by anybody but Janice's baby sister, who watched wide-eyed from her pram.

"It's a mercy she can't talk yet," giggled Janice. She went to the house and came back stealthily, carrying a doll's cradle for the kitten to sleep in and some milk the baby had left. "You'll have to buy some cat's food, won't you?" she said. "I think I can manage milk for him."

"All right," said Pauline, but she felt a little anxious. It wasn't that she begrudged spending her pocket-money on Rusty. It was just that she wondered if it would go far enough to keep her pet well fed.

While they were making Rusty play with a piece of string, there was a sudden "wuff!" in the doorway, and there stood Boris, the old retriever. Rusty arched its little back and spat bravely at the big dog, and Pauline ran to gather it to safety. But Boris only wagged his tail.

"He won't hurt Rusty. He loves kittens," cried Janice. "The cat next door is his greatest friend, and he always plays with kittens."

Sure enough, when Pauline came eagerly round to see her pet the next day, she found that the sensible little thing had already decided that the dog was harmless, and the two were frolicking together in the shed.

"I've bought a tin of cat's food," said Pauline. "It cost a lot, and I don't suppose it will last more than two days."

"The people next door buy fish-pieces for their cat. They only pay

The two were frolicking together in the shed

a few pence for quite a lot," said Janice, with a worried little frown. "But how are we going to cook fish?"

"I'll just have to save some of my dinner every day," sighed Pauline, as she watched Rusty gorging.

But she soon forgot the problem of food in her pleasure in the kitten's fun.

Her happiness in her pet only lasted a short time, however, for when she arrived at Janice's two days later she was greeted with a tale of disaster.

"Mummy knows," gulped Janice, her face still showing traces of tears. "It was Boris's fault. He pushed open the shed door and let Rusty out. Mummy was watching, and she went down the garden and found the cradle and saucer and things, so I had to tell her."

"Is Rusty safe?" was Pauline's first question.

"Yes," said Janice, "but Mummy says we can't keep him for you. She—she wants to talk to you."

"You see, Pauline," said Janice's mother, when Pauline had gone slowly in to see her, "it was wrong of you to buy the kitten when you knew your mother didn't want you to have it."

"But—but it's only because we live in a flat," faltered Pauline.

"Well, one day perhaps you'll have a garden like ours, and then you'll be able to keep a cat," said Mrs. Janes, who really meant to be kind. "Now, I think the best thing for you to do is to let me take Rusty back to the shop and ask the man to sell him for you. I'll ask him to be sure he gets a really good home. Don't you think that's best?"

Pauline nodded miserably, seeing no way out. She couldn't trust herself to speak. She told herself that she was a Brownie and mustn't cry. She dared not say goodbye to Rusty, but ran home without another glance at the ginger kitten.

She tried not to think of her lost pet during the days that followed, because, when she did, she got a horrid little ache inside her. She even avoided Janice, and was going to pass Mrs. Janes with no more than a mumble when she met her on the way to call for Janice to go to Pack meeting a week later. But Mrs. Janes stopped her with a gentle tap on the shoulder.

"Oh, Pauline," she said, with a smile, "somebody has bought your little kitten, and he's going to a home where he will be well looked after. The shopman has returned some of your money, eighteen pence of it. He kept the rest for his trouble. You'll be able to buy something else now—something your mother won't mind you having."

But Pauline didn't feel that she could buy anything else, just yet, with the money, and it was still unspent when Christmas Day came.

"A happy Christmas, dear!" said Mrs. Huggins, coming into her bedroom on Christmas morning with a smiling face. "My present is downstairs, so hurry up and dress."

"I wonder what it can be?" thought Pauline. She had one or two ideas about it, but they were nowhere near the truth, for when she entered the dining-room, after a very hurried wash and a scrambled dressing, she gave a gasp of joyous surprise.

A small ginger kitten with a large bow round its neck came prancing sideways across the floor to meet her.

"Rusty!" she cried, scooping the kitten up. "Oh, no, it can't be, it can't be!"

"Yes, it is, Pauline," smiled Mrs. Huggins. "He's my Christmas present to you."

"But, Mummy, you said——" began Pauline, scarcely daring to believe it was true.

"I know, dear." Her mother put an arm round her shoulders and gave her a hug. "I'm afraid I didn't realise how very much you wanted a pet. Mrs. Janes told me all about Rusty and you, and I bought him at once and asked the shopman to keep him for me until Christmas came. He'll just have to get used to living in a flat, I'm afraid. I spoke to the people downstairs about him, and they seemed to like the idea of a cat about the place."

With a sigh of pure happiness, Pauline put her cheek against the soft, furry little body. "I should think *anybody* would like my Rusty," she said.

And the ginger kitten purred loudly.

Veronica and the Kelpie Six

by MARGARET REED

"There goes that stuck-up new kid, Veronica Parsons." Shirley scowled after the girl who had just sailed by on a shiny new bike past the Pack meeting hall.

"Isn't she awful?" agreed Jean. "She's got a different dress for every day of the week and she's always beautifully turned out. Wonder how much pocket-money she gets."

"Bet it's three times as much as I get," said Shirley. "I can't stand the way she walks, with her nose in the air."

"And she's always talking about the things she's got," put in Sue. "It's 'I've got this' and 'I've got that'. You'd think she owned the universe."

"I feel a bit sorry for her," put in Pam. "I think she's—well, sort of lonely. She hasn't any brothers and sisters, you know."

"Lonely?" snorted Shirley. "Not her! She's too fond of herself to feel lonely. I only hope she's not in our Six when she joins Brownies."

"Brownies!" chorused the others. "D'you mean to say she's coming to Brownies?"

Shirley nodded. "Awful, isn't it? My mother met hers in the grocer's. Seems she wants her darling daughter to have friends of her own age."

"There goes that stuck-up new kid"

"That's all very well," grumbled Jean, "but what about the poor friends?"

"Well, we can't do anything about it," said Pam. "We'll just have to be as nice to her as we can."

Shirley poked her in the back. "Pam, I believe you'd try to make friends with her."

Farther down the street Veronica Parsons gripped the handlebars of her bike fiercely. She had just passed those four horrible girls. The Kelpies, they called themselves, which she was told was a Brownie Six. She hated them, especially Shirley. Shirley stared at you as if you were a worm. She said horrid things in an off-hand sort of voice, so that you didn't know whether she really meant it or was only teasing. Veronica blinked hard. She felt like crying, but she couldn't ride a bike and cry at the same time.

"Why do I find it so hard to make friends?" she asked herself. "It's always been the same. If only I had brothers and sisters! Oh, I'd give anything to belong to a Six like them, but a friendly Six." She shook her head to get rid of the tears. "I don't care," she muttered stubbornly. "I'll show them I don't care one little bit!"

The next few weeks were difficult for Veronica. Few of the girls rode bikes to school, so she went alone. No one asked her to play. Everyone seemed to have a particular chum. The more she was neglected the higher she held her head. And the higher she held her head the more stuck-up the others thought her.

In the third week in September Brownies began. Mrs. Parsons bought Veronica a uniform. Veronica eyed it with horror.

"Mummy, do I really have to join Brownies?"

"Yes," said Mrs. Parsons firmly. "I have spoken to the Brownie Guider about you. Daddy and I want you to get to know more girls, and make friends. You're too much alone. You can start tonight, dear."

Veronica turned away with a sinking heart. Mummy didn't understand. She just didn't understand.

"How can I go to Brownies with all those girls who don't care for me?" she thought desperately. "Friends! Imagine Shirley being called my friend! She could never be a friend of mine!"

Slowly she got into the uniform. She wondered uneasily whether you had to wear it on the first night. But Mummy would expect her to wear it, since she had gone to the trouble of buying it.

She lengthened out the journey as much as possible. How she hated the thought of going in! She got off at the church gate and wheeled her bike slowly up the path. Suddenly she thought of Shirley—of Shirley's mocking voice saying, "Look what's just walked in!" Panic shook her.

"I can't go in—I can't! But what will Mummy say if I go home? I'll have to ride round the streets for one hour and pretend I've been to Brownies. Anything's better than facing those horrible girls."

She swung round hastily, almost bumping into a fair girl in Brownie uniform coming up the path. The girl looked at her curiously; then she smiled.

"I say, are you a new Brownie? If so, I'll take you in."

"Well, yes," said Veronica doubtfully. "I am new."

The Brownie grinned again. "I'm Nancy. I'm the Sixer of the Sprites. You don't have to look as if you were going to the dentist. We're not as bad as all that. Come on in."

That Brownie meeting was an eye-opener to Veronica. Here the Kelpie Six didn't seem to be enemies. Even Shirley held her tongue. Veronica clung like a limpet to Nancy who helped her in every way possible. Everyone had fun, and there was a lot to learn. She rode home actually feeling happy.

"I liked it," she told her mother. "When you all wear the same uniform you feel sort of alike and it's easier to fit in—though I'm not supposed to wear the uniform until I've made my Promise."

Veronica began to look forward to the Tuesday Pack meeting as the high spot of the week. She was sorry Nancy didn't go to her school. She still had no ally there. The Kelpies seemed to have thawed only slightly towards her. Shirley was as sharp-tongued as ever. But it didn't seem to matter so much now. Veronica was doing some hard thinking.

One evening in Pow-wow Brown Owl said: "Those of you who

"Brown Owl, I've got a bike!"

were here last year will remember Mary Wilson. She had to leave because she lived too far away to get to Pack meetings, but she has missed them terribly. Her mother, who is a widow, is saving up to buy her a bike, so Mary is hoping to join us again—perhaps next year."

Veronica sat up. "Brown Owl, I've got a bike!"

Quick as a whiplash, Shirley turned on her. "Oh, of course—you've got everything!"

The Pack sat in shocked silence. Veronica's face flamed.

"I didn't mean it that way," she said shakily. "I meant I could lend Mary Wilson my bike. She comes to my school. She comes by bus, but I could easily lend her my bike on Tuesdays so that she could ride to Brownies. She could ride it from her house to school for me next day."

All the shockedness drained out of the silence. The faces turned towards Veronica were friendly and eager. A hand patted her on the back.

"Why, Veronica," said Brown Owl warmly, "that's a wonderful idea. If your mother would approve, it would solve Mary's problem till she gets her own bike. What do you think of it, Brownies?"

"It's wizard," said Pam, "but whatever will you do without your bike, Veronica?"

"I'll walk, like the rest of you. It isn't far from my house."

"That's quickly settled, then," said Brown Owl. "Yes, Shirley, what do you want?"

Shirley hung her head. "I want to say I'm sorry for what I said to Veronica. I thought—I thought she was just showing off, like she used to."

Brown Owl looked at her sharply. "I'm glad you apologised, Shirley. You would do better to think before you speak."

"But she's quite right, Brown Owl," said Veronica quickly. "I was a show-off. I know that now."

The next morning, when Veronica was getting ready for school, the bell rang. She opened the door. There stood Shirley, Jean, Pam and Sue.

"Hello, Ronnie!" said Shirley quietly. "Are you ready for school yet? We wondered whether you'd like to walk this morning." She shuffled her feet. "I mean—we wondered if you'd care to come to school with us."

Veronica stared at them. Would she care to come? Happily she shut the door behind her and fell into step with the others.

The Postponed Picnic

by ADA WELLS

Jill and Pat were twins and lived with their mother and father in a house by the sea. Their parents had decided to move into a larger house, which had to be altered before they could go and live in it.

One morning Daddy put down a letter he had been reading, looked very pleased with himself, and said, "At last the builders have finished. They say the house is ready and we can move in at any time now."

"Splendid!" said Mummy. "I'll go and measure for the curtains this morning. You two girls can come with me and see how the house looks now. You haven't seen much of it yet."

"What about the picnic with our Pack, Mummy?" asked Jill. "We're going to try and learn the crawl this afternoon."

"We'll take the food to the house and you can look over the rooms while I measure for the curtains," replied Mummy. "Then you can go down to the beach and join the others. There'll be plenty of time."

Jill and Pat put on their Brownie uniforms. Soon they were on the way to see their new home. When they reached it they went over every bit of it. The twins thought it was lovely, with plenty of space, and when they joined Mummy in the living-room, which was quite new, they were even more pleased.

"What a lovely room and what a grand view of the beach!"

exclaimed Jill, her eyes wide with excitement.

"Yes, that's why Daddy had the garage built underneath and the new room over it," said Mummy.

"Look, you can see the place behind those two big rocks where we change before we swim! Now I can see the Brownies. They're all there except us. Come on, let's hurry!" said Pat. "Oh, bother! It's started to rain."

"And the wind's getting up," said Jill. "Look at the white horses on the sea!"

"I've finished measuring now," said Mummy, coming over to them, "but you'd best wait here and see if the rain stops. If it doesn't you could have your picnic here. There are packing-cases you could sit on and you'll find the basket in the hall." As she went away, she added, "Close the window or the rain will blow in."

She hurried out. As she opened the door there was a flurry of wind. Jill, who was closing the window, thought it would be torn from her grasp. Inside, the door shut with a bang and then the window closed easily. The rain was getting steadily worse, beating on the windows and hiding the view of the beach.

"Brown Owl won't expect us until the rain stops," said Jill. "She's a super Brown Owl, isn't she? She always seems to understand."

"Yes, she does. Anyway, they've gone back to shelter somewhere now. Let's get the basket and eat our lunch; then as soon as the rain stops we can go down to the beach."

Jill went to the door and put out her hand to open it.

"Oh, gosh!" she exclaimed. "There's no door handle!"

Pat went over to look.

"How silly—only a keyhole!" she said. "It's just like an outside lock."

"Well, that's what it was. Don't you remember, Pat? There was a balcony with steps from the garden, and this door was the outside one then. I suppose the builders have forgotten to alter it. Now what are we going to do? Tell me that!"

"We'll have to climb out of the window," said Pat, opening it and looking out. "Coo! It's an awful long way down. Come and have a look. There's just nothing to hold on to. So that's no good. Now what?"

"Let's wave from the window. Someone's sure to see us."

"Don't be silly! The beach is the only place in view, and while it's pouring with rain there won't be anyone there. In any case, people on the beach couldn't see us. We couldn't see them if we were not so high up."

"I suppose not," agreed Jill, in a subdued voice. "What about our picnic? I'm so hungry and there's that basket waiting in the hall."

They looked at one another in despair. If only the rain would stop! Jill sat on a packing-case. Pat traced with her finger the raindrops running down outside the window. Soon she realised there were not so many to trace. In the sky there was a little streak of yellow light. This broadened and soon the sun was shining out over a bank of grey clouds.

"The rain's stopped, Jill," she said.

Jill looked and saw the waves rolling in, crashing on the deserted beach, catching rays of light and sparkling brightly. A strong wind was blowing the clouds away, leaving a clear blue sky. Two figures could be seen walking towards the rocks. Each had a sack, which looked to be very heavy from the way the figures were carrying them. When they reached the sea they turned their backs on the water and gazed in the direction of the road which ran down from the village. Then they went quickly behind the rocks, and for a few moments Jill and Pat couldn't see them. Soon they reappeared in the space where, as Pat has said, the girls usually changed before a swim. Now the twins could see the figures more clearly; they were two youths in denims and blue sweaters. They looked curiously about the little space, then went further on among the rocks and the twins could see them no longer.

"Wonder who they are," said Jill.

"Holiday-makers, I expect," said Pat, in an uninterested way; then in a livelier voice, "Oh, there's Molly—and Susan! Yes, and the others are coming now. I wish they could see us."

"We could tie a white shirt to a long stick and wave it until

"Oh, there's Molly—and Susan!"

someone over there notices it," said Jill impetuously.

"You are a goose! We haven't even got a shirt, let alone a white one. Our brown uniforms wouldn't be noticed even if we had a long stick to tie them to, which we haven't."

"Well, you think of something, then!" said Jill. "It's three o'clock already, but Mummy won't worry about us; she'll think we're with the others."

"It seems ages and ages since we ate," said Pat. "I'm so hungry."

Jill put her hand in her pocket and brought it out with a cry of triumph. "Look, Pat—biscuits—rather broken, but what does that matter?"

Broken or not, the twins ate them eagerly, then Pat said, "Wonder if I've got anything."

She emptied her pockets on to a case. There was a bus ticket, a piece of string and a dirty handkerchief. They each had a pocket-knife, and Jill had a Brownie Guide Pocket Book. She also added two more bus tickets and a few pieces of paper. There was certainly nothing eatable.

They wandered over to the window again. Their friends were now behind the rocks, getting ready for the swimming lesson. Undressing didn't take long, for they always put their swimsuits on underneath their uniforms. In no time at all they were ready, their clothes left in neat piles on a blanket spread on the sand. On top of the Brownie Guider's heap, although the twins couldn't see it, was a leather bag, in which the Guider carried any papers or money that she thought she might need when she took the Pack on outings. As she followed the girls, the Guider hesitated for a moment, then went back and placed the bag underneath the blanket. Then she followed the others.

"Wish we were with them. They'll know the crawl and we won't," said Pat.

"Oh, Brown Owl will understand and will be sure to teach us later. Look, there're those big boys again!" said Jill. "That's funny! Those sacks look empty now, don't they?"

Pat looked carefully and agreed. "Yes, they do," she said. "Now

With a triumphant grin he placed it in his sack

what're they doing?"

When they saw the little heaps of clothes, neatly placed on the blanket, the youths opened their sacks and started pushing the Brownies' clothes into them. They looked at the blanket for a moment, then, shrugging their shoulders moved away. One of them kicked the blanket in passing, and the leather bag was uncovered. The taller of the two picked it up and with a triumphant grin, placed it in his sack. Before going, they picked up the blanket to see if anything more was hidden underneath.

Pat and Jill watched in horrified amazement as the shorter of the two youths produced a knife from his pocket and proceeded to slash the blanket to ribbons, which he slung as far on top of the rocks as he could.

Then, with an exaggerated swing of their shoulders, the two hurried up the beach towards the road to the village.

Jill and Pat watched with growing anxiety. Was there nothing they could do to let the Brownies and their Guider know what had happened to their clothes? Soon the Brownies would be coming out of the water. They would have no towels for drying and no clothes to put on. The sun was shining, but the rain had cooled the air, and it was certainly not a warm day.

Pat picked up one of the packing-cases and carried it over to the window, intending to climb on it so that she could see more. As she set it down it toppled over and out of it fell a piece of greasy paper, probably the wrapping from someone's sandwiches.

"What time does Daddy's train come in? He's catching an earlier one today, isn't he?" she asked in a thoughtful voice.

"Yes, four o'clock. I've had an awful thought, Pat. Mummy said she wouldn't be coming here again until Tuesday. We'll be skeletons by then." Tears rolled down Jill's face.

"Of course we won't," said Pat. "Don't you remember when we were doing first-aid the other week Brown Owl said people can live on their stored water and fat for days?" But her voice was not as happy as usual, for she had just caught sight of Jill's rather skinny legs. Then she went on, more brightly. "I've just had a brainwave. If

Pat wrapped up her leg as best she could

we could light a fire in that old metal window-box and makes lots of smoke Daddy might see it on the way from the station. It might make him wonder. Anyway, we must do what we can—not only because we're nearly starving, but because we must let someone know about those two thieves. All those clothes! And some of the Brownie uniforms are nearly new."

"Oh, Pat, what a good idea about the smoky fire!" said Jill, already looking more cheerful. "We could use the packing-cases if we could break them up, but what about matches?" Pat interrupted her by suddenly dashing across the room to the fireplace. "There's a box of matches on the shelf!" she cried. "What luck! I expect the workmen left them here."

"Thank goodness they did!" cried Jill. "We haven't got much paper."

"We could use your Pocket Book," suggested Pat.

"Oh, not that!"

"Why not? You can buy another. Come on, Jill, hand it over!"

Reluctantly Jill did so and watched her sister tear the Pocket Book to pieces and place it in the old metal window-box. They added the other bits of paper, then Jill turned over the packing-case on which she had been sitting. How best to break it up? They must be quick.

"Come on, Jill! Let's jump on it!"

They jumped on the case as hard as they could. With a loud cracking sound it gave way suddenly, and there was Jill, with one foot wedged through its side.

"O-o-o, Pat, hurry!" she cried. "Get my foot out! I think it's broken!"

"The things you think!" said Pat, but, all the same, she quickly set to work to free Jill's foot. There was certainly plenty of wood now, but Jill had a nasty cut on her leg.

Jill sat on another case and Pat wrapped up her leg as best she could with her rather grubby handkerchief.

"It's a good thing Brown Owl can't see what I've wrapped up your leg with. In future I'll always have a clean handkerchief with me."

Soon thick smoke was going up

"We'd better get the fire going," said Jill. "It's nearly four o'clock and Daddy's train will soon be in."

Pat picked up a match and struck it. The flame lasted long enough for a ticket to catch alight at the edge. Hardly daring to breathe, Pat put the greasy paper to the flame. Suddenly it flared up. Pat dropped it on to the paper in the window-box, then carefully piled pieces of wood on top. Soon there was a bright fire, but not much smoke.

Jill untied the handkerchief from her leg and handed it to Pat.

"Here," she said, "try this. It should make some smoke."

She was right. Soon thick smoke was going up, obscuring the window. All they could do now was sit and wait. Together they looked out at the beach. The Brownies were just coming out of the water, making for the rocks. What would they say when they found that their clothes had gone? Soon they were in the space behind the rocks, and Pat could guess at the amazement on their faces when they found that their possessions had vanished.

Now they saw the Brownie Guider look up at the rocks and point to the remnants of the blanket. She turned to the others in what was evidently anger at the discovery of the cut blanket. For the first time, Jill and Pat realised how lucky they were that they'd not been able to go down to the beach. If they had, their clothes too would be missing.

"Oh, dear!" said Jill. "I wonder whether our signal will be seen!"

They added more wood to the window-box fire, and smoke flared up so much that they had to retreat to avoid it.

"Someone must see the signal, surely!" said Jill.

"Someone *has* seen it!" cried Pat. "Someone is coming!"

She was right. There was the sound of a door being opened below, then hurrying footsteps came to their ears. A few moments later their daddy burst in.

"Oh, Daddy, thank goodness you've come at last! We've been locked in here so long and we've had no lunch, and now, come and look. There's Brown Owl and the rest of the Pack—except us—and their clothes have been taken while they were in the water. Pat and

I saw them being taken and it was awful! We just couldn't do anything, which made it worse."

"Not so fast!" cried their daddy. "I saw fire and smoke. I thought the house was on fire."

Quickly Pat and Jill explained.

"Those two big boys. They went to the rocks where the cave is. When they came out their sacks were empty and they filled them with the Brownies' clothes and went off, laughing!" Jill's voice was full of indignation as she explained all that they had seen.

"We'd better go and see what we can do," said her daddy grimly. "The boys can't have got far. We'll be in time to catch them, I dare say. Come on!"

The two girls were only too glad to leave the room that had been a prison to them. First, they made sure that the fire in the window-box was safely out; then they followed their daddy, who drove to the police-station and reported what the twins had seen.

"Leave it to us, sir," said the police-sergeant in charge. "I know the two louts—if they're the ones that have been hanging round the village lately, as I think they must be. They won't get far."

Satisfied that the police would be able to deal with the youths and retrieve the stolen clothes, the twins' daddy hurried them home for a good meal, which both girls admitted they'd rather have even than seeing the capture of the youths.

"I'll tell the builder off about leaving a door without a handle," said Daddy. "It could have kept you prisoners for hours. As it was, it gave you a chance of using your wits in a tight situation. I must say you were very smart to think of creating a smoke-signal."

The Brownie Guider too praised the twins when she learned how they had seen the youths take the Pack's clothes and raised the alarm.

The two youths were caught by the police with the Brownies' clothes in their sacks. The youths insisted that they had taken the clothes merely for what they called "a lark", but on finding the Brownie Guider's leather bag with money in it, they yielded to temptation and kept it. The police discovered too that the sacks had

The twins followed their father to the police-station

been used for taking litter down to the beach for dumping. They hauled the youths before the local bench of magistrates, and the two were heavily fined.

The Brownie Guider was very grateful to the twins for being instrumental in saving her leather bag and its contents.

"We'll have another picnic especially for you two," she promised Pat and Jill at the next Pack meeting, "because you missed the first one."

"It was a good miss, as things turned out," remarked the Assistant Brownie Guider, and all the Pack agreed.